Growing Up!

GROWING UP!
Systemic and Neurological Independence

Copyright © 2025 by Gopal Das
All rights reserved.

Thank you for purchasing an authorized edition of this book
and for complying with all copyright laws.

For more information about using parts of this book for
commercial use, or to contact the author
for insights or appearances,
please contact the publisher at:
ryan@thegetitfactory.com.

ISBN: 978-1-953011-19-0

Soryn Publishing
An imprint of:
The Get It Factory
In association with:
WYNX: A Content Company

Salt Lake City, UT

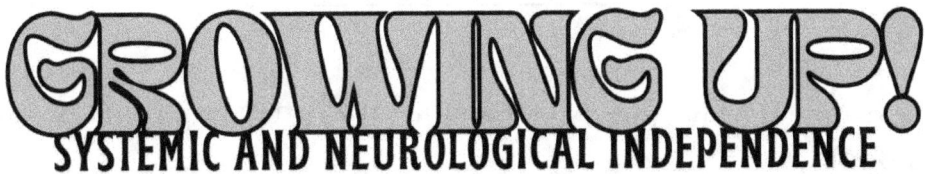

GROWING UP!
SYSTEMIC AND NEUROLOGICAL INDEPENDENCE

Gopal Das
with Gauri Devi

Publisher's Note

Full Disclosure…I May Have Accidentally GROWN UP a Little While Reading This Book

Let me start with this: I'm not a neurologist, psychologist, biologist, or any other kind of -ist that would give me a working knowledge of the inner workings of the human brain. I also don't own a meditation cushion. I'm certainly never taken any existential journeys to find myself, my purpose, or my inner peace.

I have, however, yelled out loud at my GPS, eaten half a bag of chips while staring into the fridge, and said "I'm fine" through gritted teeth while clearly being not fine. So, when my friend Gopal Das shared the manuscript of his new book called Growing Up!...(with an exclamation point, no less)…I braced myself for the usual self-help parade of buzzwords, vague encouragement, and potentially photo of someone hugging a tree.

I was so happy to be so wrong.

This book is, quite simply, different. Gopal Das uses great care and understanding of normies like me to explain the wild inner workings of the human brain. Weird doctor-y words like Profrontal Cortex, Insula, and Hippocampus are discussed in a way that actually makes sense. More than that, he does it in a way that makes you care, and want to keep reading.

As I read, I found myself imagining these brain regions like the King's Counsel in some medieval fantasy, each one arguing for my survival, my success, or occasionally, my sending a an ill-advised text message. The metaphor works for me. I even found it kind of hilarious. I love that this book will help you find your own metaphors or characters to help you work with your own brain's superheroes. But truly, I hope that you find, like I did, this book to be helpful in healing whatever battles you may be waging in your own mind.

What I love most about Growing Up! is that it doesn't ask you to become someone you're not. You don't have to wear robes or chant in Sanskrit to benefit. You just have to sit still for a bit. Breathe. Let the noise settle. And trust that your brain, with all its quirky little advisors, will do what it was already wired to do.

Yes, there's some science in these pages. But it's delivered with warmth, wit, and enough humanity that even if you can't pronounce "amygdala" on the first try, you'll still get it. And more importantly, you'll want to get more.

So, if you're feeling overwhelmed, overcooked, or just vaguely out of sync with yourself and the world around you, give this book a shot. You might just find yourself thinking more clearly, breathing more deeply, and…dare I say it…growing up a bit, too.

I, for one, enjoyed the journey. I asked Gopal Das if I could help him publish and distribute his book because I truly hope you do too.

To all souls who are seeking their true nature, the intuitive knowledge of freedom.

Acknowledgments

I would like to acknowledge all the souls who, in search of comfort and peace, have opened their hearts and shared their lives with me along this winding path—both in my personal calling and my spiritual unfolding.

To the teachers of truth and tenderness, the gurus who walked before and lit the way toward divine love and knowledge—this work is an echo of your wisdom.

With deep gratitude, I honor the living and literary influence of Ram Dass, Alan Watts, Joseph Campbell, Mark Epstein, Ph.D., and the sacred institutions that shaped me—The University of Utah and Utah State University.

To those whose presence has guided me across disciplines and dimensions—Chögyam Trungpa, Swami Chetanananda, Swami Vivekananda, Swami Hariharananda, Mr. Fred Rogers, Jesus of Nazareth, Paramahansa Yogananda, Shyam Sundar Das "Babaji", Gauri Devi, and the Goddess Saraswati, source of all creative intelligence—I offer my reverence.

To those who held space for growth and grace
in the everyday world:
The late Dr. David Groot, Dr. Jodi Morstein, Sherrie Sanchez, LCSW, Allyson Browning, LCSW, Valerie Wise Christensen, and the many teachers disguised as past partners and foster children—thank you for being part of this sacred unfolding.

To my biological family—thank you for being the original soil in which the roots of my being took hold. In the complexities and blessings of our shared life, you taught me about love, about resilience, and about the courage it takes to grow in different directions. Your presence is in my body, my voice, and my memory. I honor where we've been, and I carry your imprint with both gratitude and grace.

To my adopted family, the Jansons—thank you for opening your home and hearts to me with unwavering acceptance. Your generosity, humor, and fierce love created a sanctuary where I could soften, rebuild, and belong. You are a living example that family is not always bound by blood, but by devotion, presence, and the shared weaving of life.

To my chosen family—the dear friends who have walked with me across years, lifetimes, and liminal spaces—thank you for seeing me, challenging me, and loving me into greater wholeness. Your companionship has been a temple, your laughter a medicine, and your presence a kind of prayer that sustained me when words fell short.

To the many unnamed souls who walked beside me in silence or struggle—those who offered a kind word, a difficult lesson, a mirror I didn't expect, or a moment of unspoken understanding—your impact lives on in these pages. Even if your name is not written here, your spirit is felt in every step of this journey. Thank you for your invisible and indispensable presence.

And to the sacred texts—the Bhagavad Gita, the Bible, the Tao Te Ching, the Quran, the Dhammapada, the Yoga Sutras, the Upanishads, and the many other scriptures, sutras, and poetic revelations whispered across cultures and centuries—thank you for carrying the eternal flame of wisdom. Your words have been a lantern in my darkest nights and a compass in my moments of doubt. This offering is braided from your pages.

May this work stand as a humble
continuation of the light
you've given.

Preface
by Gauri Devi

When I first met Gopal Das eighteen months ago, I had no intention of co-authoring anything. I was working on my own project—one that emerged from nearly a decade of private healing, study, and devotion. I had spent those years piecing myself back together in the quiet way a cut heals—not by instruction, but by design. What I didn't yet know was that this meeting would become a long and surprising conversation which triangulated into this book designed for young adults learning how to look at themselves in a new way that centers them in their own compass.

As we exchanged stories—his from the trenches of psychological training and therapeutic work, mine from the lineage-less inheritance of life's hardest and most illuminating lessons—we began to find the same signal beneath different languages. What his world called neurological and systemic independence, I recognized as the spontaneous, inherent bodily remembrance of wholeness—a re-sensing of one's place in the great field of things by learning to tune into your own instrument.

My life didn't lead me through clinical studies or formal academic credentialing in the traditional sense. Instead, I spent more than three decades on the other side of that system—learning from deep within it. As a woman, as a mother, as a lifelong chaplain in the truest sense, I've accompanied people through the hardest passages of life: death, birth, rupture, repair. I've spent years in intensive therapy, not just for myself, but in support of children, partners, and families—each of us at some point given a diagnosis, a label, a treatment plan. I've walked through the full terrain of what that system can offer and what it can't. It has been teacher, mirror, cautionary tale—and, at times, a kind of spiritual initiation.

So while I don't speak from institutional authority, I do speak from deep and lived authority—the kind you only gain by walking with people through grief, chaos, and return. I carry a feminine lineage of wisdom that wasn't ordained or credentialed, but it has never failed me. It's the kind that emerges, like all natural things do, when the conditions are right.

And over this past year, I've had the privilege of witnessing Gopal's gifts firsthand. As a therapist, he offers something rare and vital: the ability to mirror people back to their own courage, to help them soften tight perspectives and begin to move again. I've seen his clients uplifted and empowered without dependency, finding new space to grow. He carries a deep presence and a playful precision that allows people to feel safe enough to reimagine themselves.

What emerged through our ongoing conversation—his psychological models shaped by fifteen years of experience, and my inner approach shaped by decades of devotional, somatic, and ecological inquiry—was a practical and powerful synthesis, one especially suited to young adults learning how to inhabit themselves in a time of widespread uncertainty. He gave shape to something I hadn't yet named, and in doing so, opened a new door for young adults seeking their own true north.

This book is a beautiful and unexpected result of that synthesis. It reflects his lens and language, but the medicine here belongs to no one. It belongs to all who remember how to listen. It belongs to those willing to unplug from the noise and come back into rhythm with something deeper, slower, and more true than any system, doctrine, or diagnosis could ever offer.

If you read nothing else but this preface, let me leave you with this:
The healing you long for is already moving in you. It is biological, ecological, rhythmic, and self-verifying.

You are not a project. You are not a pathology. You are a participant in a much larger harmony.
And when you turn toward that—gently, curiously, consistently—you'll begin to feel it.
Not as a belief. As a pulse.
And from there, you'll know what to do.

I'm glad you found this book and offer you my confidence that everything you need for a beautiful life lies within you when you simply make time to listen.

—Gauri Devi

INTRODUCTION

Welcome to Freedom (And a Little Chaos)

True Independence:
The Freedom to Choose Your Own Path

"Systemic" and "neurological" independence might sound like terms straight out of a neuroscience textbook, but in reality, they are deeply personal—and profoundly life-changing frameworks. At their core, they are about reclaiming your ability to live with true freedom, clarity, and intention. They are about no longer being a puppet to external systems or your own unexamined mental habits.

We live in a world overflowing with distractions, contradictions, and instant gratification. Information floods our minds at every turn. The sheer variety of choices and beliefs can feel overwhelming, and yes—the world, in many ways, is falling apart as it has many times before. But here's the truth: you don't have to fall apart with it.

Be an active participant, instead of endlessly reacting to the chaos around you. You don't have to live at the mercy of outdated systems, toxic narratives, or the collective anxiety of a world that thrives on fear. Instead, you can cultivate a level of inner resilience so strong that no external force can shake your sense of self.

You aren't ignoring reality or pretending that suffering doesn't exist. It's about growing up in a way that allows you to move through life without being controlled by it. It's about your innate ability to choose which beliefs, systems, and influences deserve space in your mind and which ones you release. Imagine creating a life where outside chaos doesn't puncture your bubble—not because you're oblivious, but because you've built something stronger than fear. That's pretty groovy and liberating!

This kind of independence is necessary. And the moment you start to cultivate it, you step into a power that no system, no belief, and no external circumstance can take away from you.

This book is a lighthearted, simplified interpretation of insights and concepts drawn from cultures, philosophies, and practices around the world. My goal is to help you grow spiritually, psychologically, and emotionally in a way that feels practical, measurable, and most importantly—fun.

This book is for you. It's about finding your way to thrive, savor life, and stop being held hostage by your past or anxious about your future. The ideas I'll share don't require blind faith or any loyalty to any belief system. They're self-evident and self-verifying, and they'll prove themselves through your own experience. All I ask is that you approach this with curiosity and the willingness to "grow up" in the truest sense.

Right now, take a deep breath and notice: Are you thinking about what you just read, or did your mind drift to something external? That's your brain running on autopilot. Feel free to take some notes or doodle what your mind does. This book will teach you how to take back control.

That petri dish? It's a perfect metaphor for my life. My mind was like agar for other people's chaos. I absorbed the emotional toxins of everyone around me (what some would call being empathic) and hoarded them on top of my own baggage. Imagine a mind so full of mess it resembled a doomsday stockpile—complete with metaphorical toilet paper.

But here's the twist: while my mind became a breeding ground for others' messes, it wasn't just their emotional junk I collected. I also soaked in the beautiful parts of their energy—love, joy, wisdom, creativity, and hope. Just as a petri dish can host both harmful bacteria and beneficial microorganisms, my mind also became a repository of others' best qualities. I gathered the kindness, the laughter, the moments of insight, and the bursts of inspiration that came from those around me. It wasn't just the shadows I took in; I welcomed the light too.

Cleaning up that mess—sorting through the emotional toxins while preserving the goodness—has been my life's work. And if I can do it, trust me, you can too. The key is learning how to filter what stays and what goes, to discard the junk and nurture the beauty that others have shared with you. It's an ongoing process, but it's possible to transform that petri dish of chaos into a vibrant ecosystem of growth and balance.

What about you? What unexamined emotional "bacteria" have you been carrying? What thoughts, fears, or expectations are lingering in your mind—not because you chose them, but because you absorbed them? And most importantly, which ones are actually serving you?

This book is about developing the tools to clean up that petri dish—to cultivate a mind that isn't just reactive to its environment, but consciously shaping it. Because once you learn how to filter the noise, you begin to create a life that's truly yours.

The Journey to Loving the Mess

Today, I can honestly say I love every part of my journey. That doesn't mean it was easy or that I escaped without scars. It means I've stopped seeing my struggles as personal attacks or unshakable burdens. They've become lessons.

My stories in this book aren't about proving my expertise or showing off some heroic narrative. They're here to inspire hope. You don't have to be trapped by the pain of your past or the pressure of your future. You can grow up—beyond your narratives, beyond your systems, and beyond the things that feel like cages right now.

The systems that shape us—parents, religion, society, the internet—aren't our fault. But they're not excuses either. By discovering your own unique True North, you can escape the domestication of these forces and sail toward the most epic version of yourself.

Street Cred

Look, I could rattle off a list of fancy credentials, but let's be real—that's not why you're here. What actually matters is that I've spent years in the trenches, walking alongside people just like you, helping them untangle the mental loops, outdated scripts, and external noise that keep them stuck. The real question isn't about my background—it's about how these insights can help you step into a level of independence that no system, no belief, and no past conditioning can take from you.

What My Internships Taught Me

All of my acquired credentials are nice, but my internships? Those were the beginnings of real education. Let's start with the first one: a hospital in the Salt Lake Valley.

I was placed in the Women's Pavilion, a setting I initially felt out of place in as a man. My role was to support NICU and Labor and Delivery units—spaces where life and death coexist. Watching tiny lives grow in incubators until they could go home with their caregivers was awe-inspiring. But I also faced moments of immense grief, as parents confronted the fragility of life in ways no one can prepare for.

During that time, I had the profound experience of co-facilitating the hospital's grief and loss group with another soulfully deep colleague. Week after week, we sat with individuals whose lives had been irrevocably altered by loss—some sudden, some expected, but all deeply felt. In those sessions, we witnessed firsthand the immense difficulty people have in accepting the finality of life. No matter their background, beliefs, or age, there was a common thread: an unshakable attachment to the idea of immortality, even when faced with undeniable evidence that life is, by nature, impermanent. It was both humbling and eye-opening to see how fiercely we cling to the notion that death is something to be resisted, something unnatural, rather than an integral part of the human experience.

This resistance to mortality runs deep, woven into cultural narratives, religious doctrines, and personal fears. In many ways, we live in a world that avoids honest conversations about death, treating it as a distant concept—something to be postponed, battled, or even denied altogether. And yet, in doing so, we rob ourselves of a fundamental human right: the right to live and die peacefully. What I learned in that grief group was that much of the suffering surrounding loss isn't just about the absence of a loved one; it's about the unresolved relationship we have with mortality itself.

Later in this journey, we will take a deep dive into the realities of life and death—not from a place of fear, but from a place of inquiry, acceptance, and, ultimately, liberation. We will explore the lost wisdom surrounding the art of dying well, a concept that many ancient traditions embraced but modern society has largely forgotten. By investigating our cultural conditioning, our personal fears, and the ways in which we can reclaim a more peaceful relationship with our own impermanence, we may find that understanding death more deeply is the very thing that allows us to live more fully.

My second internship placed me in the heart of a deeply stigmatized, impoverished school—a place where childhood was often overshadowed by violence, instability, and systemic neglect. Many of the children I worked with were caught in the crossfire of gang rivalries, domestic struggles, and the crushing weight of poverty. Their stories were not just statistics; they were lived realities. Day after day, I sat in classrooms and walked the hallways, witnessing firsthand how trauma took root in young minds. Their nervous systems were constantly on high alert, their bodies primed for survival rather than learning. They weren't just struggling academically—they were navigating a world where safety was not a given, and trust was a fragile, fleeting thing.

Among the staff, lunchtime conversations frequently revolved around abuse, neglect, and heartbreaking situations no child should ever have to endure. Many of the adults, though well-meaning, were drowning under the emotional weight of their environment. Frustration, burnout, and despair loomed heavy, and it was easy to see how even those with the best intentions could fall into cycles of reactivity rather than responsiveness. But in the midst of all this, my supervisor stood out—a calm, steady presence, a bright light who refused to let the chaos dim her shine.

What made her different? She didn't get consumed by the dysfunction around her. She didn't meet chaos with more chaos. Instead, she operated from a place of deep awareness and emotional regulation. She responded rather than reacted. She embodied a level of neurological independence that allowed her to lead with wisdom rather than impulse. And that, I realized, was the key.

How are children supposed to access true development when the adults around them are stuck in survival mode—operating from the most primitive parts of their brains, reacting instead of guiding, mirroring dysfunction rather than modeling resilience? From a broader perspective, many of these adults (myself included) were not behaving in a way that reflected their full potential for maturity and wisdom. Instead, they were stuck in patterns of emotional reactivity, unwittingly reinforcing the very cycles they sought to break.

This realization is crucial because it invites a powerful question: How often do we, as adults, operate from our most reactive, primitive selves rather than from a place of awareness and growth? Whether we are teachers, parents, leaders, or simply individuals navigating our own lives, the way we show up and grow up matters—not just for ourselves but for those who look to us for guidance.

This book will explore the profound connection between emotional regulation and true self-governance—how the ability to rise above reactivity and meet adversity with clarity is not only a skill, but a responsibility. If we wish to create environments where growth, learning, and healing are possible, we must first cultivate that same environment within ourselves. We cannot demand emotional maturity from children, students, or employees if we are unwilling to embody it ourselves.

True development—whether personal or societal—begins when we step out of survival mode and into conscious awareness, choosing to lead with wisdom rather than fear.

Why Therapy Needs a Rethink
Honoring Progress While Acknowledging Gaps

Let's be honest: therapy, as it's often practiced, has both incredible strengths and significant blind spots. First, the majority of those needing support cannot afford therapy. Second, the deep wisdom required to counsel the wide array of the human experience cannot be effectively conveyed to 20 year olds in a classroom. Third, even when one has means to access quality therapy, Western psychology—for all its groundbreaking advancements—has in some ways drifted into an imbalance. It can focus so deeply on analyzing the past that it may forget to equip people with practical tools to navigate the present and shape the future.

This isn't to say that therapy is ineffective—far from it. Modern psychology has revolutionized our understanding of trauma, attachment, and neuroplasticity. We now know more about the brain, emotions, and the nervous system than ever before. However, where therapy often falls short is in its tendency to overemphasize excavation over integration. It's invaluable to understand how our past has shaped us, but if the process stops at insight alone, then people are often left with knowledge of their wounds but no real tools to heal them.

Here's what I've observed (and lived): When people share their darkest, most painful stories in a dysregulated state—when they're overwhelmed, activated, and emotionally raw—it doesn't necessarily free them. Instead, it strengthens those neural pathways, cementing the trauma even deeper into their psyche. This is not just an anecdotal observation; neuroscience supports it. Repeatedly reliving a traumatic experience under heightened emotional distress doesn't resolve the trauma—it reinforces it, solidifying the pain rather than dissolving it.

I've seen well-meaning therapists encourage clients to pour out their most painful memories, mistaking catharsis for transformation. And I've seen fresh-out-of-grad-school therapists beam with pride when a client breaks down in tears, believing that "getting to the root" of their suffering means they are finally making progress. The therapist feels validated. The client feels temporarily relieved. And for a fleeting moment, it seems like a breakthrough. But here's the million-dollar question: **Then what?**

Understanding where your pain comes from is only the first step. Often we as therapists wonder once the session is over if we have actually equipped our clients with actual tools to regulate their nervous system, shift their emotions, and handle life's inevitable ups and downs. Traditional therapeutic training has focused so heavily on analysis and insight that it has sometimes neglected the practical application of healing.

And that's the gap. *Catharsis is not healing.* Catharsis without integration is like opening a deep wound and just staring at it, expecting it to close on its own. Yes, you've exposed it—but now what? Therapy that focuses solely on "getting to the root" without teaching the body and mind how to regulate, rewire, and respond differently is like giving someone a diagnosis without offering a cure.

People don't just need to understand their pain—they need to transform their relationship with it. This means moving beyond just talking about emotions to actively engaging in practices that help rewire the nervous system, shift perception, and create new experiences of safety and agency.

Where Western Psychology Advanced Where It Got Stuck

Western psychology has come incredibly far in recognizing the complexity of the human mind, trauma, and behavior. We've moved beyond simplistic models and now understand how neuroplasticity allows the brain to rewire itself, how the nervous system plays a huge role in emotional regulation, how trauma isn't just psychological—it's stored in the body, and how attachment patterns shape our relationships. These are massive contributions to human understanding and healing.

However, even with these insights, psychology has developed a blind spot: it often overemphasizes analysis and insight while underemphasizing embodiment and integration. Traditional talk therapy often assumes that if you just understand why you feel the way you do, you'll naturally start feeling better. But anyone who has been stuck in therapy for years will tell you—knowing why you feel a certain way doesn't necessarily help you stop feeling that way.

This is where neuroscience offers an important truth: the mind doesn't heal by endlessly replaying old pain—it heals by creating new experiences. This is not to say that diving into childhood wounds or reflecting on past traumas is useless—it's actually incredibly valuable. However, insight alone does not automatically lead to change. Healing happens through rewiring the nervous system to respond differently to triggers, developing new behavioral patterns that reinforce safety and agency, integrating past experiences without being dominated by them, and living in the present rather than endlessly analyzing the past.

In essence, healing isn't just about understanding pain—it's about teaching the brain and body how to relate to it differently.

A New Approach: Skills Before Stories

This is why I take a different approach and encourage openness to working just a little differently. Instead of immediately diving into the deepest, most painful memories, we first build skills, stability, and emotional resilience. We create a foundation of regulation before ever touching the heavy stuff.

Why? Because when people learn how to regulate their emotions, how to shift their mental state, and how to break free from automatic reactions, something powerful happens. They no longer feel controlled by their past. The traumas that once haunted them lose their grip. And more often than not, they realize they don't even need to go back and relive every painful memory—because they're too busy actually living.

This is about reclaiming the present. When someone strengthens their ability to regulate their nervous system, reframe experiences, and shift their emotional state, they naturally change their relationship with their past without needing to endlessly relive it.

This is what true healing looks like. Not just understanding trauma, but moving beyond it. Not just talking about emotions, but learning how to shift them. Not just reliving the past, but building a future that isn't dictated by it.

Western psychology has given us many tools—it just needs to emphasize integration and embodiment as much as it emphasizes insight and analysis. Therapy isn't broken. But to truly empower people to heal, it needs to evolve—moving from a model of endless excavation to one of active transformation.

The Only Place Healing Happens: Right Here, Right Now

One of my guiding teachers, Ram Dass, said it best: "Be Here Now." It's the only place we actually exist. It's the only place where we have any influence over our perception of life.

Think about it:

- *The past? It's just a story you tell yourself that has deceased.*

- *The future? It's pure imagination not yet born.*
- *But the present? That's where the magic happens and is living.*

When we stop obsessing over "fixing" the past and start focusing on mastering the present, everything changes. Instead of spending years in therapy searching for a breakthrough, people learn how to create one for themselves—right now, in this moment.

And that is true healing.

"True healing only happens in the present moment." Reflect on a time when letting go of the past or fear of the future allowed you to experience a breakthrough in the now. How did being fully present shift your perception, your choices, or your sense of self?

Regarding Neurospicy Kids and Adults

Let me tell you about one of the greatest joys of my life: working with neurodivergent kiddos and adults—what I affectionately call the neurospicy. These individuals are extraordinary. Their honesty, creativity, and unfiltered emotions bring an authenticity to the world that many of us spend a lifetime trying to reclaim.

For 15 years, I ran Camp Takoda, a summer treatment program designed specifically for neurospicy children. Later, I founded Chiron Academy, a fully accredited school built to meet their unique needs. In the midst of these chaotic but deeply meaningful experiences, I also had the privilege of fostering two incredible boys—both with long lists of diagnoses and externalized behaviors. And let me be clear: they and their families were my greatest teachers. These experiences reinforced a lived experience that even with the wildest diagnosis, each child had a magical world of their own that deserves to be honored and expanded beyond labels. Not to back into a society that doesn't support them, but to magnify their own neurology that benefits their experience in the world that is full of love and non-judgment.

At Camp Takoda I was able to de-escalate even the most heightened crisis, having been forged in the fires of chaos myself. I wasn't afraid of these kids because I knew what it felt like to be out of control, to have a nervous system that refused to cooperate. They could sense that.

I was growing by observing them. I had spent my childhood learning to perform, please, and blend in, and these kids had a chance to live unfiltered, unapologetic lives. Their emotions—anger, sadness, joy—were raw, real, and true. It wasn't always easy, but it was always honest.

Chiron Academy was my attempt to create something better—a space where neurospicy kids and their families could thrive academically, emotionally, and socially. For five years, it was magical. It was also wildly exhausting. And then the pandemic hit, forcing the school to close. It was devastating. But it also made me face something I had been avoiding: the parts of myself that still needed healing.

And that's why I care. Not just because I see the brilliance in these kiddos, but because I know firsthand what it's like to fight against a world that doesn't always understand you. They deserve a space to be seen, supported, and empowered. And so do you.

Burn It All Down (Again)

After Chiron Academy closed, I found myself standing in the rubble of everything I thought defined me. My career, my relationships, my sense of purpose—it all felt like it had collapsed. So, I did what anyone in a midlife existential crisis might do: I sold my beautifully remodeled home, bought an old Mercedes Winnebago, and hit the road with a powerful sage and healer, Gauri Devi, I'd recently met through the Utah Chamber Artists.

For months and months, we traveled. We studied spirituality, philosophy, neurology, and Western psychology with the kind of intensity you'd expect from people who were trying to rebuild their life from the ground up. I personally wasn't looking for answers so much as I was looking for clarity. I'm so grateful I had grounded company, otherwise I would have surely succumbed to padded walls and a cocktail of medications. We learned that this life truly is a group project in order to see parts of ourselves that can't be accessed just by looking in the mirror.

Eventually, my travels led me to Ohio, where I stumbled upon a derelict Presbyterian church. It was crumbling, forgotten, and in desperate need of care—kind of like me at the time. But something about that old church spoke to me. I bought it, and as I work to restore its beauty, I find myself restoring my own sense of purpose.

While my path involved radical shifts, yours doesn't have to. Whether it's changing your routine, questioning old beliefs, or simply pausing before reacting, small steps lead to big independence.

You're the Hero

Here's the truth: You don't need saving—you never did. Every single person is on their own path of self-discovery, but no two journeys look the same. I can't give you what you need, nor would I ever claim to. Only you can do that. What I can offer are tools, insights, and perhaps a little encouragement to remind you of what you already know deep down: that you are capable, that you are enough, and that you were always meant to walk this path in your own way.

If you've been carrying the weight of the world on your shoulders, hear this: you don't have to. You don't need to fix everything. You don't need to save everyone. You don't need to have all the answers. All you need is the courage to turn inward, to meet yourself fully, and the willingness to grow—not into someone better or more worthy, but into the fullest, truest version of yourself.

"You were never meant to be rescued—you were meant to remember your own strength."

Write about a moment in your life when you realized no one else could save you. How did that realization empower you? What did it teach you about your own capacity to grow, heal, or lead?

Congratulations, Dear Traveler

Not for finishing this book—not yet—but for something far greater: for stepping onto the path that, paradoxically, you have never left.

You see, the moment you even considered taking this journey, you had already arrived. The door was never locked. The map was always in your pocket (check, it might be crumpled under some old receipts). And now, here you are—not a beginner, but a long-lost master simply remembering your own wisdom.

This is radical, isn't it? The realization that enlightenment is not some distant, mythical peak to conquer, but the very ground beneath your feet? That the journey isn't about collecting spiritual merit badges, but about noticing the luminous, chaotic, imperfect perfection of this moment—including your unwashed coffee mug, your unfinished to-do list, and yes, even that slightly embarrassing thought you just had.

So, I bow to you. Not as someone who has it all figured out (heaven forbid!), but as a fellow traveler who is delighted to meet you here, in the only place we could ever meet: right now.

"The journey was never about arriving—it was about remembering." Write a letter to your past self from the perspective of the "long-lost master" within you. What gentle truths would you share? What would you remind yourself about the path, the purpose, and the quiet wisdom that's always been yours?

A Commitment to Presence

So, let's make a humble commitment—not to perfection, but to curiosity. Not to fearing life, but to stepping toward it with a little more courage. Not to chasing some final arrival, but to meeting each moment with an open heart, a sense of wonder, and just enough laughter to keep things interesting. And let's commit to documenting this journey, so that when doubt arises (as it inevitably will), we can flip back through the pages of our own evolution and remember:

We are growing. We are learning. We are becoming.

Since you have already arrived, there is only one thing left to do: keep going—and document everything.

Growth is continuously unfolding. Not because you are not lacking, but because Life Itself is movement. The ocean never holds a single wave in place. The tree never decides it's "enlightened enough" to stop growing. And so, too, you will keep evolving—not toward some imagined ideal, but toward the ever-deepening truth of who you already are.

But here's the key: if you don't document your growth, you may not realize how far you've come.

The Science of Journaling and Self-Reflection

Modern neuroscience confirms what sages have long understood: writing things down changes the way the brain processes experience. When we document our journey—our thoughts, emotions, struggles, and breakthroughs—we create a record of our own transformation. Journaling is not just a tool for self-expression; it's a mechanism for reprogramming the brain, reinforcing new patterns, and making sense of our evolving selves.

Consider this:

- *Writing activates the brain's reticular activating system (RAS), helping you notice patterns and insights that might otherwise go unnoticed.*

- *Journaling strengthens neuroplasticity, the brain's ability to rewire itself, by helping you shift from reactive emotions to conscious reflection.*
- *Studies show that documenting thoughts and feelings reduces stress, improves emotional regulation, and increases self-awareness—all essential components of true personal growth.*
- *When you look back at past journal entries, you can track your evolution, recognize recurring themes, and see proof of how you've changed—even in moments when it feels like you haven't.*

In essence, documentation grounds your progress in reality. It prevents your mind from playing tricks on you, from making you believe you're stuck when, in fact, you've been moving forward all along.

So let's begin. Not by waiting for the perfect moment, but by stepping into the only moment that has ever mattered—this one. Are you ready?

"Journaling isn't just reflection—it's transformation in motion." Begin by writing a short entry titled "Where I Am Right Now." Describe your current state—emotionally, mentally, spiritually—without judgment. Then ask yourself: What am I learning? What patterns am I noticing? What am I being invited to change or embrace? Let this be a snapshot of your evolution in real time.

Curiosity is Key

So, let's make a humble commitment—not to perfection, but to curiosity. Not to fearing life, but to stepping toward it with a little more courage. Not to chasing some final arrival, but to meeting each moment with an open heart, a sense of wonder, and just enough laughter to keep things interesting. And let's commit to documenting this journey, so that when doubt arises (as it inevitably will), we can flip back through the pages of our own evolution and remember: We are growing up!

So let's begin. Not by waiting for the perfect moment, but by stepping into the only moment that has ever mattered—this one.

Are you ready?

"What would happen if I approached my life with curiosity instead of judgment?" Write about a situation you're currently facing—or one that's been lingering—and explore it through the lens of wonder rather than worry. What questions arise when you stop trying to "figure it out" and instead choose to listen to what life is showing you?

CHAPTER 1

A Ministry Without Dogma

**A Spiritual Exploration
Rooted in Freedom and Understanding**

My fascination with spirituality has been woven into my life for as long as I can remember. From a young age, I felt a deep sense of divine presence, a quiet yet undeniable protection that defied logic. It wasn't something I could explain, but it was always there, guiding me, anchoring me in moments of uncertainty. In recent years, however, this exploration has evolved. It has deepened beyond simple belief and into a more profound inquiry—one that isn't about following prescribed doctrines but about uncovering the universal truths that transcend religion, culture, and time.

I am captivated by the essence of spirituality—the wisdom that has been passed down through various traditions, not as rules to obey but as insights that help us connect to something far greater than ourselves. What interests me are the patterns, the repeating messages that emerge across faiths and philosophies. These aren't just abstract ideas; they are profound tools for transformation. I firmly believe that understanding these universal truths is key to both systemic and neurological independence.

When we explore spirituality without attachment to any one system, we gain access to a vast library of wisdom that helps us navigate life with more clarity and freedom. Sometimes, a single story from a culture or tradition completely different from our own can illuminate a truth more powerfully than anything else. That's why I pull from a wide range of spiritual philosophies, psychological frameworks, and neurological research in my work. I don't just accept ideas at face value—I double-check them against what we now know about the brain and how humans develop resilience, contentment, and joy.

I am interested in self-creation—the idea that every person has the ability to design their own inner world, to craft a life that aligns with their deepest truth. By developing systemic and neurological independence, self-creation becomes tangible.

My goal is simple but vast: to help infinite types of people to access infinite paths to joy, connection, peace and Life Itself. Because the path is never one-size-fits-all. There is no single way to find fulfillment, no universal roadmap to enlightenment. That's the beauty of it. You don't need someone else's permission or approval to seek what feels right for you.

What I can do is guide you toward discovering that the answers were inside you all along. The power, the wisdom, the connection—you already have it. My role is simply to remind you that you are the creator of your own experience, and the journey toward inner freedom is yours to shape.

"What does spiritual freedom mean to me?" Reflect on your personal journey with spirituality—how it began, how it has evolved, and what it looks like today. In what ways have you moved beyond external systems or expectations? What universal truths have stood out to you along the way, and how have they shaped your sense of inner freedom and self-creation?

Reframing "God":
A Non-Dogmatic Understanding of the Divine

The word God is heavy. It carries the weight of history, of devotion, of centuries of both reverence and dogma. For some, it is a source of comfort, a presence that has always been near. For others, it is a word entangled with rules, expectations, and the pain of feeling separate or unworthy. And for many, it is a word that no longer fits—a garment tailored for another time, another understanding.

But what if we set the word aside for a moment? What if, instead of trying to define the indefinable, we simply looked for the experience of what people have called God—the pulse of something greater, the quiet presence behind all things?

For me, the answer has always been there, waiting in the simplest of places: in the way the sun rises without asking for permission, in the rhythm of breath filling and emptying the body, in the way the ocean refuses to hold a single wave in place.

This is why I call it **Life Itself**.

"What happens when I let go of the word 'God' and simply seek the experience?" Explore your personal relationship with the idea of the divine—however you define it (or don't). How has your understanding evolved? What moments or experiences have connected you to something greater than yourself, beyond names or doctrines? What does Life Itself feel like to you?

Life Itself Is Not Separate from You

Somewhere along the way, we were taught that God is something outside of us—above us, beyond us, watching us from a distance. A being separate from creation, sitting in judgment or offering rewards. But how could this be, when every breath we take is a testament to something greater moving through us?

Look around. There is an intelligence that turns acorns into towering oak trees, that orchestrates the quiet miracle of your heartbeat, that transforms a single cell into an entire human being. This same intelligence flows through the rivers, through the wind, through the tiniest creatures that dance unseen beneath the soil. It is not an entity standing apart from existence—it is existence itself. And if it is in the trees, and in the stars, and in the oceans, then it is in you too.

You were never separate from it. You have been breathing in the sacred since the moment you arrived here.

Write down a couple of things that provoke awe and see if you can find connections between the amazing and yourself. You are not separate but included in the amazing tapestry of Life Itself.

Life Itself Is Awareness

Perhaps what people call God is not a being at all, but a state of being. A presence. A vast, silent awareness that has always been with you, watching without judgment, waiting without urgency. It is that stillness you feel when the mind quiets, the soft hum beneath the noise of thoughts.

Have you ever stood in nature and felt something shift inside you? Have you ever looked at the sky after a storm and felt, without words, that you were a part of something infinite? That awareness—that felt sense of belonging to something far greater than yourself—needs no name. It simply is.

And yet, when you touch it, you know. Not in the way we know facts or information, but in a deeper, wordless way. This is why sages, poets, and mystics across traditions have struggled to explain it—because it cannot be taught, only experienced.

Life Itself Is Connection

If you strip away the theology, the scriptures, and the doctrines, what remains at the heart of every spiritual tradition? Love. Not as a fleeting emotion, but as a fundamental force that binds all things together.

Maybe what people call God is not a distant ruler, but the space between us—the warmth of an embrace, the unspoken understanding between two people, the way strangers come together in times of crisis. It is the invisible thread connecting every living being, reminding us that we are not alone.

It is why we grieve when someone we love is gone—because love itself is evidence that we are woven into something much greater than ourselves.

"If God is not a being, but a presence—an awareness, a connection—how have I experienced it?" Reflect on moments in your life when you felt a profound sense of belonging, stillness, or love that needed no explanation. How did those mo-

ments shape your understanding of divinity? What happens when you let go of definitions and simply feel your way into the mystery of Life Itself?

Finding Your Own Language for the Sacred

Words will always fall short when trying to define something as vast as the divine. That's why I do not insist on the word God—because we can experience something broader, something that speaks more clearly to the experience of what we know to be true for ourselves. Whatever label you use, it is supposed to be highly personal to you.

Life Itself is the clearest way to describe what is sacred. It is the force that moves through all things. It is the intelligence that beats within the smallest seed and the most distant star. It is the awareness within us and the love between us. It is the miracle of breath, the gift of presence, the great unfolding of existence itself.

This is not about what I call it. It is about what you call it, about how you experience it. Whether you find it in nature, in music, in the eyes of someone you love, or in the silence of your own heart—whatever name you give it, whatever shape it takes—what matters is that you feel it.

Because Life Itself has always been here. Waiting. Moving. Living. And it has never been separate from you.

"What is my personal language for the sacred?" Take a moment to reflect on your unique experience of the divine—beyond names, traditions, or expectations. Where do you feel closest to Life Itself? What words, images, or metaphors naturally arise when you try to describe that connection? Let this be an exploration, not a definition.

CHAPTER 2

Systematic Independence

Systemic independence is the exhilarating moment you realize you are not just a passive passenger on the conveyor belt of life—you are the driver, the navigator, the architect of your own path. It's not about breaking free from all systems (because, let's be honest, you still have to pay bills, obey traffic laws, and occasionally pretend to enjoy small talk at family gatherings). Rather, it's about waking up to the invisible scripts you've been handed—the "shoulds" and "musts" that shape your decisions—and deciding, with clarity and courage, which ones actually align with who you are.

Imagine the power of stepping outside the default settings of your life. Instead of chasing approval, tradition, or the latest algorithm-driven trend, you begin to move with intention. You start questioning: Do I really want this job, or was it just the "safe" choice? Do I actually believe in this lifestyle, or did I absorb it from my surroundings?

The beauty of systemic independence is that it doesn't mean rejecting everything—it means reclaiming your agency. It's the moment you stop being unconsciously shaped and start shaping yourself.

And yes, it can be uncomfortable at times. Breaking free from autopilot means taking responsibility for your choices, and that's both liberating and terrifying. But it also means stepping into a life where you get to define success, happiness, and meaning on your own terms. It means realizing that you are more than a collection of societal expectations—you are a thinker, a creator, an independent force in a world that desperately needs more conscious and intentional people.

So go ahead, question, choose, and carve your own way. The systems will still be there, but now you decide how much power they get to have over you. This is in fact part of growing up!

"Which invisible scripts have I been living by—and which ones am I ready to rewrite?" Reflect on the beliefs, roles, or societal expectations that have shaped your decisions so far. Which ones feel authentic? Which feel inherited, outdated, or imposed? What does it look like to step into your own definition of meaning, success, and freedom?

Why It Matters

Authenticity

Navigating the world's expectations is like being in a never-ending talent show where you don't remember signing up. One minute, you're trying to fit into a trendy aesthetic (minimalist? maximalist? cottagecore??), and the next, you're nodding along in a conversation about crypto even though you still don't know what blockchain actually is. Systemic independence is what helps you step off that stage and say, "Wait, do I even want to be in this competition?"

It's the difference between wearing a certain outfit because you love it and wearing it because an influencer convinced you that "quiet luxury" is your new personality. I guess what I'm trying to say is that when you stop letting external pressures dictate your every move, you might find that your true self was way cooler than the version you were trying to manufacture.

"Where in my life am I performing—and what would it feel like to stop?" Think about areas where you've felt the pressure to conform, impress, or fit in. What would it look like to drop the act and show up as your unfiltered self? What parts of you have been waiting quietly for permission to be seen, heard, and expressed authentically?

Personal Responsibility

Realizing you have control over your own choices is like discovering a secret level in a video game you've been playing on autopilot. Holy Cow, it's so cool that you're your own boss! Suddenly, you see doors you didn't even know existed. You can choose to step away from obligations that drain you. You can embrace a new hobby, even if it feels out of place. You can gently remove yourself from spaces that no longer serve you.

It's empowering, but with that power comes a deeper responsibility. The hard truth is that when you find yourself stuck, or repeatedly agreeing to things that make you unhappy, it's no longer something or someone else's fault. It's on you. And once you embrace that responsibility, life begins to feel less like a series of unfortunate events and more like something you can gently guide with your own hands.

And with that shift, it's important to let go of old narratives that keep you tethered to the past. We all carry the marks of our upbringing, and it's okay to acknowledge the ways in which our past shaped us. But at some point, we must realize that we are no longer children. We are capable of writing our own stories. It's time to release the need to blame our parents or circumstances for where we are today. They did their best with what they knew, just as we are doing our best now.

The journey to healing and growth begins with the gentle recognition that you have the power to change the story, to let go of the past, and to step into your own strength. It's not about perfection, but about choosing to grow up, and trusting that you have everything you need to move forward.

"What story am I ready to stop telling—and what story do I want to write instead?" Reflect on a belief or narrative you've carried that may have once protected you, but now holds you back. How has it shaped your decisions or identity? What shifts when you take full responsibility for your choices, and begin to author your life from a place of strength rather than blame?

Balance

Finding balance is like trying to carry groceries in one trip—you can do it, but it requires strategy. You don't have to drop your career, social life, and responsibilities to become some enlightened, system-free being who lives in the woods and communicates only via interpretive dance. You just have to remember that these things shouldn't define your entire identity. Yes, you can be ambitious without making your job your entire personality. You can nurture relationships without sacrificing your alone time. You can even—brace yourself—log off social media without the world forgetting you exist. Systemic independence is knowing that you can engage fully without being swallowed whole.

"Where in my life am I over-identifying—and what would balance look like instead?" Explore the areas where you've merged too tightly with a role, title, or external identity. What parts of you have been overshadowed in the process? What would it feel like to show up fully without being consumed? Define what balance means for you—not as perfection, but as a sustainable rhythm that honors all parts of who you are.

How to Develop It

Self-Reflection

You ever have one of those moments where you suddenly realize you've been following a completely arbitrary rule for years? Like thinking you have to eat three meals a day at the "right" times, or that pineapple on pizza is a crime (it's not—it's just misunderstood). Self-reflection is about questioning why you do things and deciding if they actually serve you. Maybe you went to law school because your family expected it, but deep down, you'd rather be designing video games. Maybe you've been forcing yourself to like yoga because it sounds healthy, but honestly, you just want to go on long, dramatic walks while listening to 90s music. The goal isn't to burn everything down—it's to make sure what you keep is yours.

"What rules have I been living by that I never actually agreed to?" Think about the routines, beliefs, or choices that have shaped your life. Which ones truly reflect who you are—and which ones were inherited, absorbed, or assumed? What would your life look like if you let go of the ones that no longer serve you and kept only what feels genuinely aligned?

Mindful Consumption

Have you ever spent 20 minutes scrolling through social media and then realized you suddenly need a $75 water bottle, a new skincare routine, and a trip to Iceland? That's not you talking, that's the algorithm whispering in your ear like a shady salesman. Mindful consumption means recognizing that everything you take in—books, news, conversations—shapes your thoughts. It's the difference between reading something that genuinely inspires you versus something that just sends you into a spiral of inadequacy.

So if a podcast makes you feel like you're failing at life, mute it. If your morning doom scrolling leaves you in a bad mood before you've even had coffee, reconsider. The world isn't going to stop feeding you information, but you get to decide what's on your mental menu.

"What's on my mental menu—and is it actually nourishing me?" Take stock of the media, conversations, and content you regularly consume. How do they make you feel? Which ones expand your sense of possibility, and which ones shrink it? What might shift if you became more intentional about the information you allow into your mind and heart?

Simplify Where Possible

Overcommitting is like trying to juggle flaming torches while riding a unicycle—it may look impressive, but eventually, something is bound to catch fire. In the rush of daily life, we often find ourselves caught up in the illusion that the more we do, the more worthy or accomplished we become. But the truth is, life becomes infinitely lighter and more fulfilling when we make the conscious choice to remove the unnecessary.

Simplification doesn't mean radically altering your life or dropping everything that brings you joy and purpose. It doesn't mean quitting your job to live in a van (unless, of course, that's the adventure your heart craves—then, by all means, embrace your inner nomad). It simply means learning to discern between what you genuinely want and what you've been conditioned to say yes to out of obligation.

How often do we find ourselves RSVP-ing to events that drain us, attending social gatherings not because we desire connection, but because we feel we should? Or maybe we're paying for streaming subscriptions we barely use—how many times have you scrolled through them only to realize that you always go back to the same two shows? Simplifying isn't just about decluttering your space; it's about decluttering your time and energy. Maybe your weekend doesn't need to be filled with errands, re-organizing every corner of your home, meal-prepping for the week, and trying to keep up with every message in your inbox.

In fact, when we stop and listen, we can hear a quieter, more profound truth: our minds, bodies, and souls need space to breathe. The practice of systemic independence doesn't always come through big, dramatic decisions. It often shows up in the small, daily choices that give us back our time, space, and sanity.

Systemic independence isn't about rejecting everything you've been taught or taking an extreme stance on minimalism. It's about waking up to the realization that you don't have to blindly follow the script you were handed. You don't need to keep playing the same role you've been cast in. You have the power to edit the script, rewrite it, or, when needed, toss it aside and start fresh with a new approach that's more aligned with who you truly are.

Life becomes infinitely richer when you begin to craft it consciously, moment by moment. And if you slip back into old habits, don't be too hard on yourself. Life has a way of gently nudging us back on track. Simply laugh at the folly, adjust your course, and keep moving forward—this time, more attuned to your own terms.

When I traveled to India to explore the paths of many spiritual adepts, I had the privilege of spending time with a Sadhu (a wandering ascetic) at his ashram. What struck me wasn't his words or teachings—it was his stillness. He wasn't striving to prove anything, seeking validation, or performing spirituality. He simply existed, with an unshakable presence that drew people toward him without effort. His lesson included the simple wisdom of the following statement: "Simple Life, Good Life. Good Eating, Good Sleeping, Good Pooping."

In a world obsessed with proving worth through constant action, this was a revelation: True systemic independence isn't about running away from systems—it's about being so deeply rooted in your own clarity that external forces no longer dictate your sense of self. You don't need to abandon society or live in a monastery to cultivate this. It starts wherever you are—by simplifying, by questioning your defaults, and by learning to sit with yourself without distraction.

This is the gift of simplicity—it doesn't need to be complicated to be powerful. The quieter, more mindful moments often reveal the most profound truths. When we remove the excess noise, we can hear our hearts and minds more clearly, and in that silence, we find our true direction.

"What am I carrying that I don't need—and what would it feel like to set it down?" Reflect on the commitments, routines, or expectations in your life that may be weighing you down more than lifting you up. What are you saying yes to out of obligation, habit, or fear of judgment? If you gave yourself full permission to simplify, what would stay, what would go, and what space might open up for your truest self to breathe?

5 Self-Verifiable Ways to Practice Systemic Independence (Today, Right Now)

Systemic independence is about recognizing and reclaiming control over the external influences that shape your decisions, habits, and behaviors. These five self-verifiable challenges allow you to test your level of independence in real time, revealing just how much outside forces dictate your actions—and how you can start breaking free. Let's have courage to grow up by practicing systemic independence in the following ways.

After completing these challenges, reflect on which ones felt the hardest and what they revealed about your unconscious habits. Practicing systemic independence isn't about rejecting everything—it's about making conscious choices instead of acting on autopilot. The more you test your independence, the stronger it becomes.

1. Go a Full Hour Without Checking Your Phone

Your phone is a direct pipeline to external influence—social media trends, news cycles, constant communication, and other people's expectations. If you can't resist the urge to check it, who's really in control? Set a timer for one hour and avoid touching your phone—no scrolling, no notifications, no quick checks. Pay attention to any discomfort: Do you feel anxious, bored, or restless? If so, consider what this says about your dependency on digital input. Successfully completing this challenge reveals how much control you have over your attention.

Be brave and write down your honest experience!

2. Say "No" to Something You Don't Want to Do (Without Justifying It)

Many of us instinctively explain or over-apologize when we decline something, as if simply not wanting to isn't a valid reason. The next time someone asks you to do something you don't want to do—whether it's attending an event, taking on extra work, or answering a call—say, "I won't be able to." Resist the urge to explain. Notice both the other person's reaction and your own emotional response. If you feel guilty, ask yourself why you feel obligated to justify your boundaries.

Could you actually do it? How did it go?

3. Make a Decision Without Asking for Anyone's Input

Constantly polling others before making choices—whether it's picking a restaurant, an outfit, or a weekend plan—suggests you might be outsourcing your autonomy. Today, make a simple decision entirely on your own, without asking for validation. Did you hesitate or second-guess yourself? If so, why? Practicing small acts of decisiveness strengthens trust in your own judgment.

Write down your process and feelings you experienced. Make sure to include your wins along with any struggles.

4. Unfollow or Mute One Source of Influence That Doesn't Serve You

The content you consume directly shapes your thoughts and emotions. If an account, news source, or social media trend consistently makes you feel inadequate, anxious, or drained, it's influencing you more than you realize. Take a moment to scroll through your feed, identify one such source, and mute or unfollow it. If this feels difficult due to fear of missing out or guilt, that's proof of just how deeply digital influences control your mental space. Notice if your mind feels clearer afterward.

Which source did you decide to cut? Why? What do you expect will happen over time without this influence readily availalbe to you?

5. Spend 15 Minutes Alone Without Any External Input

We are constantly consuming—music, podcasts, texts, social media—rarely sitting in pure silence. Set a timer for 15 minutes and simply be—no phone, no TV, no distractions. Go for a walk, stare at the ceiling, or sit quietly with your thoughts. Observe your reaction.

Does silence feel peaceful or uncomfortable? Do you immediately crave stimulation? If the quiet unsettles you, ask yourself why and write it down.

Chapter 3

Neurological Independence

What It Is

Neurological independence is about freeing yourself from the loops of your own mind— freeing yourself from the mental cages society tries to build around you. In today's world, there's a tendency to slap labels on every thought pattern, every emotion, every quirk of the mind. Sometimes, labels like anxiety, ADHD, ASD, or depression can serve as a helpful starting point for understanding our minds. They give us language to describe our experience, a sense of connection to others who feel the same way, and, for some, relief in knowing we are not alone.

But here's where things get tricky—labels can also become cages. If we aren't careful, they shift from being descriptions of what we experience to definitions of who we are. 'I have anxiety' turns into 'I am an anxious person,' and before we know it, we start shaping our identity around something that was never meant to be permanent. The truth is, your brain is capable of adaptation, rewiring, and change—far beyond any diagnosis you may have received. So rather than rejecting labels, ask: "Are they guiding me toward growth, or are they keeping me stuck in a script I didn't write?"

Neurological independence teaches you to see beyond these limiting definitions and recognize that your brain is fluid, adaptable, and capable of transformation. It doesn't matter what name someone has given your particular set of thought patterns—you have the ability to shift them, to rise above them, to create new mental pathways that serve you rather than trap you. You are growing and maturing your own software constantly.

Traditional therapy has given us incredible tools—greater awareness, emotional validation, and, for many, life-saving support. But here's where we've gone off course: the idea that endlessly digging through the past is the only path to healing. The idea is to balance self-reliance and professional support. Imagine you're in a car, trying to reach a destination, but instead of driving forward, you spend all your time analyzing the road behind you. Sure, the road tells you how you got here, but at some point, you have to grab the wheel and start moving. Therapy is invaluable, but it should also teach us how to build new thought patterns, re-wire our responses, and step into the driver's seat of our minds. Because real healing doesn't just happen in reflection—it happens in action.

While traditional therapy offers valuable insights, it often falls short in teaching people how to reprogram their minds for real freedom. Rather than empowering people to transcend their mental patterns, it reinforces the idea that they are victims of their own minds. It tells people they are sick, disordered, and in need of lifelong management rather than recognizing the mind's extraordinary ability to heal and evolve. It profits off suffering, keeping people dependent on endless therapy sessions and medications instead of guiding them toward true freedom. This approach often does not liberate—it perpetuates suffering by making people identify with their struggles instead of teaching them how to master their own consciousness.

We don't pretend that struggle doesn't exist. It's about refusing to let those struggles define you. When you step back from the label-driven thinking that western psychology imposes, you start to see that you are not a problem to be solved. You are a conscious being, capable of growth, healing, and self-mastery. Neurological independence puts you back in the driver's seat. It lets you say, "Yes, my mind does certain things—but I am not powerless here. I can train it, guide it, and shape it into something that supports my highest self." And that, my friend, is true freedom.

Write down some of your own attachments to labels beyond mental health diagnosis. How does the label of being a son or daughter, child, friend, etc., add or distract from the entirety of who you are?

Why Neurological Independence Matters

Clarity of Mind

When you're not drowning in the endless commentary of your own thoughts, life becomes a lot simpler. Without all that internal chatter—rehashing the past, worrying about the future, arguing with imaginary people in your head—you start to see reality as it actually is. Clarity of mind isn't just about feeling peaceful; it's about being able to respond to life intelligently, rather than being swept away by every emotional wave. It's the difference between standing firmly on solid ground versus being tossed around in a mental hurricane. When your mind is clear, decisions come easier, challenges seem more manageable, and Life Itself feels lighter and lucid.

Ever had a moment where you're frantically searching for your keys, flipping over couch cushions, emptying out your bag, accusing innocent bystanders of theft—only to realize they've been in your pocket the entire time? That's what it's like to live with a noisy mind. It complicates everything, making even simple situations feel overwhelming. But when you cultivate clarity, it's like suddenly remembering to check your pocket first. The chaos quiets down, and life becomes far easier to navigate.

"What clears the noise in my mind—and how can I create more of it?" Think about the moments when your mind feels most calm, clear, and spacious. What helps you access that clarity—whether it's nature, movement, silence, or creativity? Where in your life is mental clutter clouding your perception, and what gentle shifts could help you return to your inner stillness more often?

Emotional Resilience

Most people assume emotions just "happen" to them, like unpredictable storms. But what if you could be the sky instead of the storm? Emotional resilience means recognizing that your habitual emotions—whether it's anger, fear, self-doubt, or anxiety—are not permanent fixtures in your being. They are patterns, and patterns can be rewired. When you develop neurological independence, you stop being at the mercy of these old emotional loops. Instead of instantly reacting with frustration, worry, or self-sabotage, you create space. That space allows for a choice: do I feed this emotion, or do I redirect my energy toward something that actually serves me? Over time, the emotional turbulence settles, and a more stable, peaceful way of being takes its place.

If you've ever stubbed your toe on a table leg and felt an immediate, irrational fury—not just at the table, but at the entire universe—you've experienced what it's like to be ruled by emotions. One small incident and suddenly you're spiraling into rage, questioning why furniture even exists. But when you build emotional resilience, you don't get swept away so easily. You stub your toe, you acknowledge the pain, and you move on.

"What emotions tend to hijack me—and what might it feel like to be the sky instead of the storm?" Reflect on an emotional pattern that often takes over—anger, fear, anxiety, etc. What typically triggers it, and how do you usually respond? Imagine what might shift if you could create a pause between the trigger and your reaction. What would it look like to meet that emotion with awareness instead of reactivity?

Freedom from "Autopilot"

Most people are living their lives on autopilot, reacting to whatever life throws at them without much awareness. Someone cuts them off in traffic? Immediate anger. A coworker makes a passive-aggressive comment? Instant resentment. Their phone buzzes? Mindlessly checking notifications for the tenth time in an hour. But what if you didn't have to be a puppet to every external trigger? Neurological independence gives you back your power.

Instead of being yanked around by impulses, you learn to pause. To choose. To decide how you want to show up at each moment. This is real freedom—not just external freedom, but internal sovereignty over your own mind.

Have you ever picked up your phone to check one email, only to resurface two hours later, deep in a conspiracy theory about how birds aren't real? That's autopilot. One small impulse leads to an unconscious chain reaction, and suddenly you have no idea how you got where you are. But with awareness, you can break the spell. You can see the urge arise, recognize it for what it is, and make a conscious choice—put the phone down, take a breath, and reclaim your attention before you spiral into the pigeon matrix.

Most of us have had a moment—big or small—that shaped how we see ourselves, often without realizing it. Maybe a teacher told you that you weren't creative, and suddenly, you stopped drawing. Maybe a parent casually said you were 'bad with money,' and years later, you still hesitate to make financial decisions. For me, it was a simple, offhand comment about being too affectionate when I was younger. That one sentence planted a seed of self-doubt that took years to unroot. The point isn't that we should blame these moments; it's that we need to recognize how much power they hold. When we bring awareness to these subconscious scripts, we get to decide whether we still want to follow them.

"Where in my life am I living on autopilot—and what might awaken me?" Identify an area where unconscious patterns tend to run the show—how you react to stress, how you use technology, how you speak to yourself. What mo-

ment or belief from your past may have shaped this response? If you could pause and choose a new way of being, what would it look and feel like to reclaim your awareness and rewrite the script?

How to Develop It

Meditation & Mindfulness: An Introduction

Meditation is not about turning your mind into a blank void. It's about noticing how your mind works and gently reclaiming control. Something as simple as focusing on your breath for a few minutes a day can start to loosen the grip of old thought patterns. At first, your mind will resist—jumping from one distraction to another, as if it's allergic to stillness. That's normal. The point isn't to stop thinking; the point is to notice when your mind wanders and bring it back. This simple act of returning is what builds the muscle of awareness. Over time, you'll start to see the gaps between stimulus and response widen, and in those gaps, you'll find your freedom. You breathe in, You breathe out.

If you've ever sat down to meditate and suddenly remembered every unfinished task from the past decade—Did I ever text Sarah back in 2017? Where is my birth certificate? Did I leave the oven on?—then congratulations, you've experienced the universal struggle of meditation. Your brain, desperate to avoid stillness, will throw every possible distraction at you. But the magic happens when you realize you don't have to chase those thoughts. You can simply notice them and return to the breath. And little by little, that awareness starts to spill over into daily life, helping you break free from reactivity.

I once had the privilege of meditating in a cave along the Ganges in India, a place that carries centuries of sacred history. At first, I expected something dramatic—some grand revelation or spiritual lightning bolt. But what actually happened? Silence. A deep, unwavering stillness that, for the first time, made me realize just how much noise I was carrying in my mind. That's when it clicked—awakening isn't about seeking some external sign. It's about peeling away the distractions and finally listening. You don't need to travel across the world for that kind of clarity. You just need to create the space to notice it.

What are some of the experiences that you have had when life seemed to uplift you? Write down some of your game changing events in your own life.

Conscious Movement

Your body and mind are not separate entities. They are deeply intertwined, communicating with each other in ways we often don't fully realize. The tension in your body fuels the tension in your thoughts, and in turn, your mental stress manifests physically. How often do you find yourself tightening your shoulders, clenching your jaw, or holding your breath during moments of stress or anxiety? These physical responses are not isolated—they are the body's way of echoing the emotional state you're experiencing. Practices like yoga, tai chi, or even mindful strength training teach us to listen—to really tune in to the signals our bodies are sending.

Where am I holding stress? What physical habits are linked to my emotional reactions?

When you begin to move with intention—whether through slow, deliberate yoga poses or through focused, controlled exercise—you start to develop an intimate relationship with your body. This awareness becomes a bridge between mind and body. For example, you might realize, "Ah, my shoulders always tense up when I'm stressed" or "I hold my breath when

I feel anxious." This recognition is transformative, because it offers you a new pathway to break old patterns—not just mentally, but physically. With conscious movement, you can begin to untangle not only the knots in your muscles but also the knots in your mind.

If you've ever tried yoga, you've probably experienced the sensation of being trapped in a pose that made you question all your life choices—one leg trembling, your arms shaking, silently praying for the moment when you can release and collapse onto the mat. That's the body's tension coming to the surface, and it's often when we feel the most uncomfortable that the body is releasing what it has been holding onto for so long. But here's the beautiful thing: when you release physical tension, your mind follows. It's not just about stretching—it's about untangling the emotional and mental knots that have been stored in your body. Through conscious movement, you create the space for both your body and mind to let go, relax, and find equilibrium.

My personal practice of conscious movement over the past decade has taken the form of indoor rock climbing. The beauty of climbing, much like yoga or tai chi, is that it demands total presence—your attention must be anchored to every movement. There is no room for distractions; the consequences of losing focus can lead to injury. I recall one particular session with a friend where we were both working on a challenging route, one we'd been attempting for a few days. I had made progress on my own with the route at the gym. When we finally climbed together, I was eager to show her that I had completed it. As I ascended, I moved fluidly—everything felt easy and effortless. I was about to top out when, for some inexplicable reason, I decided to mansplain the climbing problem to her—while still on the wall.

At that moment, I lost my focus. As I was speaking, I neglected my foot placement, and in a split second, my toe slipped off the hold. The next thing I knew, I was sliding down the rough slab, like a soft cheese scraping against a cheese grater. I landed awkwardly on my ankle, injuring myself in the process and sidelining my climbing for a couple of weeks. It was a sharp reminder of how deeply intertwined mind and body truly are. One lapse in awareness, one moment of losing focus, and the physical consequences followed.

That experience taught me, in no uncertain terms, that conscious movement is the key to not just physical success but to emotional balance. The body and mind, when aligned through awareness, can achieve remarkable things. But when we stray from that alignment—even for a moment—things can quickly spiral out of control.

So whether it's through climbing, yoga, or another mindful practice, the essence of conscious movement is presence. When we move with awareness, we allow our bodies to heal, our minds to clear, and our spirits to find balance. It is through this union of mind and body that we begin to unlock deeper levels of understanding—not just of ourselves, but of the world around us. When you learn to move with intention, you create harmony both within and without.

"How does my body reflect my inner world—and what happens when I move with intention?" Think about a physical practice or moment of embodied awareness—whether it's climbing, yoga, dance, walking, or even just breathing deeply. What emotions, memories, or insights surface when you're fully present in your body? How has conscious movement helped you untangle mental or emotional knots, and what has it taught you about the relationship between awareness and healing?

Self-Inquiry

Most of us have been running the same mental programs for so long that we don't even question them. But when you start asking, Why do I think this way? What triggers me? Where did I learn these patterns? You open the door to transformation.

Try this:

1.   *Write down a belief you have about yourself.* ('I'm bad at public speaking,' 'I'll always struggle with money,' 'I can't trust people.')

2. *Ask yourself where it came from.* Was it a personal experience? Something someone told you? A cultural expectation?

3. *Challenge it.* Is it 100% true? Can you find a time when the opposite was true?

4. *Reframe it.* What's a version of this belief that empowers you instead? ('Public speaking is hard for me, but I can improve.')

5. *Test it.* Next time you catch yourself repeating the old belief, replace it with the new one and notice what happens.

Self-inquiry is like shining a flashlight into the dusty corners of your mind, illuminating beliefs and reactions that have been operating on autopilot. Journaling, contemplation, or even discussing these questions with a trusted friend can be incredibly powerful. The more you investigate, the more you interrupt old mental loops, and the more space you create for new, intentional ways of being.

Have you ever reacted way too dramatically to something minor—like a friend teasing you—and then spent hours thinking, Wait, why did that hit such a nerve? That's the beauty of self-inquiry. Instead of assuming, "I'm just overly sensitive," you can dig deeper and discover, "Oh wow, this reminds me of when my third-grade teacher told me I'd never be good at spelling." And once you see the pattern, you're no longer trapped in it. You get to rewrite the story—and finally forgive your third-grade teacher for their unnecessary hostility toward silent letters.

Developing neurological independence is not about "fixing" yourself—it's about realizing you were never broken to begin with. You have always had the power to shift your mind, to break free from old patterns, and to cultivate a life of clarity, resilience, and true presence. It starts with awareness. It deepens with practice. And before you know it, the monkey mind that once ran the show begins to settle, leaving you with the one thing you've always had but rarely noticed—your own inner peace.

Five Self-Verifiable Ways to Practice Neurological Independence (Today, Right Now)

Time to grow up! Neurological independence isn't about controlling every thought—it's about recognizing that you are not at the mercy of your own mind. Your brain runs on habitual patterns, often dragging you through loops of worry, distraction, and automatic reactions.

The good news? You can interrupt these patterns, and these five challenges will prove it to you in real time.

By practicing these five challenges, you prove to yourself that you are not at the mercy of your brain's automatic patterns. Every time you test your neurological independence, you gain more control over your mind and reactions. The more you experiment, the more freedom you create

1. Interrupt a Thought Pattern (Right Now)

Your mind constantly runs thought loops, often unnecessary ones—like suddenly remembering an embarrassing moment from years ago. Right now, take a moment to notice what your brain is doing. Are you overanalyzing, worrying, or daydreaming? Interrupt it. Say "stop" in your mind, take a deep breath, and consciously shift your focus. To test this further, set a timer for 60 seconds and try to think about nothing—just observe your breath. Watch as your mind tries to sneak in random thoughts. Catch them, bring your focus back, and laugh at the predictability of your brain.

Write or doodle about your experience.

2. Delay Reactivity by 3 Seconds

Most of our reactions are pure reflex—someone cuts you off in traffic, and anger flares up instantly. But what if you inserted a three-second pause before responding? Try this physically first: Clench your fist tightly for five seconds, then slowly open it. That sensation of tension and release is exactly what happens when you create space before reacting. The next time someone irritates you—whether it's a slow walker in front of you or a frustrating email—pause for three seconds before responding. This tiny pause may prevent unnecessary frustration or regret.

What shifts did you feel in your hand? What do you expect would happen when you're irritated?

3. Catch a Sensory Autopilot Moment

Your brain filters out most of your surroundings, running on habitual perception. Right now, take a moment to notice something new in your environment that you usually ignore. Maybe it's the faint hum of an appliance, a small scratch on your desk, or a subtle smell in the air. By consciously redirecting your senses, you override autopilot mode and heighten your awareness. To test this further, walk into a familiar room and challenge yourself to find five things you've never noticed before. Suddenly, your environment feels sharper and more alive.

Could you find five things? How do you think your brain operating in autopilot mode affects you?

4. Break a Small Habit—Just to Prove You Can

Your brain loves routine, even for minor actions like brushing your teeth with the same hand or sitting in the same chair. Breaking even a small habit proves that you are in control, not just running on automatic. Cross your arms and notice which hand is on top. Now switch them. Feels weird, right? That's because your brain has an ingrained preference. Choose a simple habit today—like using your non-dominant hand to brush your teeth, open doors, or stir your coffee—and break it. At first, your brain will resist, but then it will adapt. That's proof that you can rewire habits anytime you choose.

Which habit do you plan to change? What do you expect to feel? Come back to this page and leave thoughts of your experience.

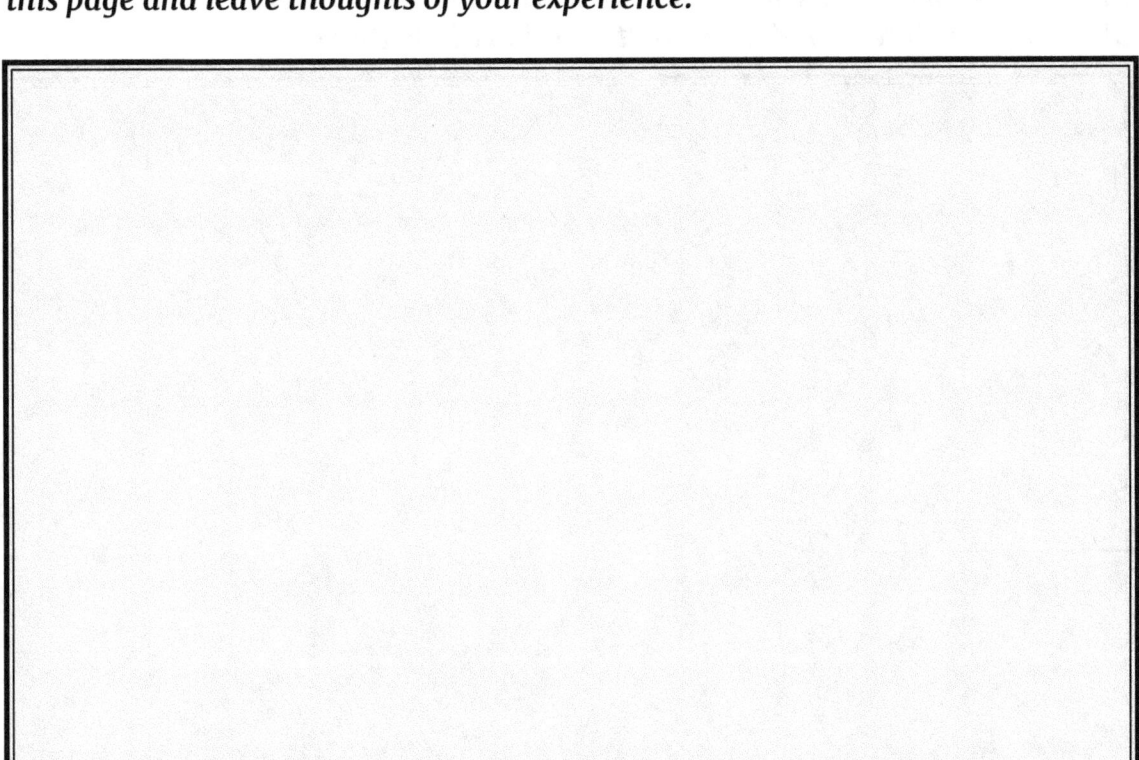

5. Label a Thought Without Identifying With It

When a negative thought appears—like "I'm so behind on everything"—you usually believe it, spiraling into stress. But what if you labeled it instead? Instead of being consumed by it, say, "Ah, that's an anxiety-thought" or "There's my perfectionism again." Suddenly, you've created distance between yourself and the thought. You're not inside it—you're observing it, like a scientist studying a wild specimen. To test this, the next time a negative or distracting thought pops up, name it instead of engaging with it. Try saying it in a goofy voice for extra effect. Notice how labeling the thought weakens its grip.

Record your experience. Which negative thought did you label? Was it easy to identify? What did you call it? Did you feel a wane in its power? For fun, you can also draw a before and after characterization of the thought.

FREE SPACE!
Record any thoughts, questions, concerns...or just take break and draw a snowman.

CHAPTER 4

The Power of Combining Systemic and Neurological Independence

Here's the reminder that true freedom is not just an abstract idea or something you read about in a self-help book and nod along to—it is a living experience, an integration of body, mind, and spirit that allows you to move through life with clarity, balance, and maybe even a little bit of grace (or at least fewer accidental faceplants and ankle sprains).

Most of us, however, live caught in a tug-of-war. On one side, we have the external world—family expectations, cultural conditioning, social pressures—all of them subtly (or not so subtly) shaping how we think, act, and see ourselves. On the other side, we have our own inner world—the mental loops, emotional reactions, and deeply ingrained habits that make us say, Why did I do that again? True freedom is when we realize we don't have to be yanked around by either one. Instead, we learn to see both clearly, step out of the game, and walk our own path with a sense of ease (and maybe a little style).

Systemic independence is about understanding that the world will always have its rules, expectations, and sometimes downright bizarre social norms (like why do we apologize when someone bumps into us?). It's not about rejecting society or moving to a remote cave—although when you're stuck in traffic, that option might sound tempting. Instead, it's about developing an awareness of how these external forces operate so they no longer dictate your choices. When you have systemic independence, you engage with the world, but you're no longer unconsciously playing by rules that don't align with your deeper truth. You stop living for the approval of others, and you start living with intention. And the best part? You don't have to wear itchy metaphorical masks anymore—you get to be fully, unapologetically yourself.

Neurological independence, in its essence, is about finding harmony with the mind—sometimes unruly, often dramatic, and always full of endless chatter. If systemic independence is the art of not letting the world dictate your choices, neurological independence is the skill of not allowing your own thoughts to hijack the narrative of your life, like an over-caffeinated director on a power trip.

Have you ever found yourself lying awake at 2 AM, trapped in a thought spiral, convinced that you've ruined your life because of a cringe-worthy moment from middle school? That's exactly what we're talking about. The mind can be a relentless, mischievous trickster, replaying old mistakes or anxieties until we start to believe them.

Back to systemic and neurological independence, the mind is a creature of habit, and it thrives on repeating patterns—fear, doubt, worry, comparison—over and over again, until we believe these thoughts as absolute truths. But the power of neurological independence lies in realizing that we don't have to take every thought so seriously. Many of us hold back parts of ourselves because of fleeting moments from the past. But when we practice awareness and self-compassion, we reclaim those parts of ourselves.

Neurological independence is the ability to observe your thoughts with clarity, to recognize their fleeting nature, and then choose which ones are worth your time and attention (spoiler alert: most are not). Instead of letting old mental patterns hold you hostage, you cultivate the ability to create space within your mind. This space allows you to respond, not react. It allows you to remain grounded, even when life feels chaotic.

The peace you create isn't one of perfect calm where nothing ever disturbs you. No, it's a deeper peace, the kind where you can stand amidst the storm and still feel okay. Even when life swirls with uncertainty, you've built an inner anchor that keeps you steady, knowing that, despite the noise, you are whole, you are enough, and you have the power to choose your response.

Now, here's where the magic happens. When you bring these two types of independence together, you start navigating life in a way that feels deeply authentic. You're no longer on autopilot, bouncing between external expectations and internal anxieties. Instead, you move through the world with clarity, purpose, and—dare I say it?—a little bit of joy.

You stop wasting energy on unnecessary mental battles, and you start channeling it into what actually nourishes you. Your awareness expands, your choices become intentional, and you begin to experience a deep, unshakable sense of freedom. And when that happens, something funny occurs: you laugh more, you stress less, and you find yourself enjoying the small, simple moments that you used to rush past. Even waiting in line at the grocery store becomes an opportunity to just be—instead of an existential crisis about whether you picked the wrong checkout lane.

Now, I know what you might be thinking: Does this mean I have to give up all my worldly attachments and become some kind of detached, enlightened sage? Absolutely not. True independence is about showing up more fully. It's about being engaged, but from a place of steadiness rather than reactivity. You don't have to give up your relationships, your work, or your favorite TV shows (yes, neurologically independent people can enjoy Netflix, too). You simply learn to engage with all of it with a greater sense of freedom—less burdened, more present, and, let's be honest, way more fun to be around.

Because here's the thing: real freedom isn't about avoiding the messiness of life. It's about learning to dance with it. It's about being able to sit in the middle of chaos and still feel at peace, to experience challenges without being consumed by them, to love deeply without being afraid of loss. When you cultivate systemic and neurological independence, you step into a life where you are no longer bound by invisible chains—whether they come from the outside world or from inside your own head. You realize that joy is not something you chase; it's something that naturally arises when you are free. And purpose? It's not something you have to go out and find—it unfolds effortlessly when you are living from a place of true presence.

You don't need to escape difficulties—just meet them with awareness. The moment you pause and choose your response instead of reacting automatically, that's freedom in action.

"What does freedom mean to me when I stop chasing it and start living it?" Reflect on a time when you felt caught between external expectations and internal thought loops. What shifted when you paused, noticed, and chose a new response? How do systemic and neurological independence show up in your life—and what might it look like to embody both more fully? Write about the version of yourself who navigates life with clarity, ease, and presence—not because life is perfect, but because you're showing up on your own terms.

Honoring Roots, Embracing Growth: The Freedom to Choose Your Own Path

For many of us, our upbringing—whether cultural, religious, or familial—has given us a strong foundation. But real growth isn't about blindly following or rejecting those influences. It's about making them your own. Maybe you were raised with certain beliefs that still feel true for you—that's beautiful. Maybe some teachings no longer resonate—that's okay too. Independence is about asking, 'What do I choose to carry forward?' Honoring your roots doesn't mean you can't evolve—it means you engage with them with awareness, gratitude, and intention.

Does cultivating this kind of independence mean I am dishonoring my parents, my religious beliefs, or my ancestors? Absolutely not. In fact, true independence allows you to honor them more deeply—not out of blind obligation, but from a place of genuine understanding and gratitude. Many of us were raised with deep respect for tradition, family values, and faith, and these can be beautiful, grounding forces in our lives. But when we follow them automatically, without reflection, we risk living someone else's script rather than discovering our own authentic relationship with these teachings. Independence is not about rejecting where you came from; it's about consciously choosing how to integrate those influences in a way that aligns with your own path.

Think of it this way: your ancestors, your parents, and your spiritual traditions all had their own journeys, shaped by the times they lived in, the challenges they faced, and the wisdom they gathered. They made choices based on what they knew and what they believed was best. And now, you are here, with your own life to live. Honoring them does not mean copying their every step—it means carrying their wisdom forward while also allowing yourself to evolve. It means embracing the values that truly resonate with you while also questioning, deepening, and refining your own understanding. This is growth.

True independence is choosing how to integrate your roots into your unique journey. And our ancestors? They were seekers, just like us. They adapted, they learned, they made mistakes, and they kept going. If anything, breaking free from unconscious conditioning is one of the greatest ways to honor them. It means we are continuing the journey, not just repeating the past.

So independence is a profound way of saying, "Thank you for all that you have given me. I carry your wisdom in my heart, and I also honor my own unique path." When approached with humility and sincerity, this kind of freedom does not separate us from our roots—it deepens our connection to them, allowing us to engage with them not out of fear or obligation, but with love, awareness, and deep reverence.

"What do I choose to carry forward—and what am I ready to transform?" On the next page, reflect on the cultural, familial, or spiritual roots that shaped you. Which teachings or values still resonate deeply, and which ones feel ready to evolve? How can you honor your lineage while also forging your own path? Write from a place of gratitude and clarity, exploring how you can weave tradition and transformation into something wholly your own.

CHAPTER 5

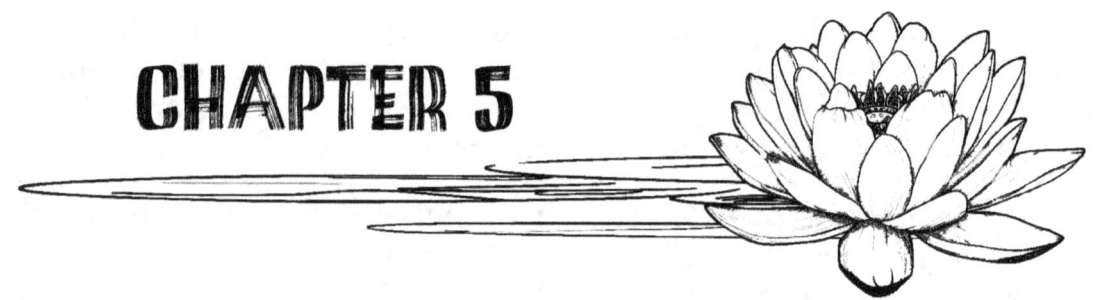

Getting to Know Your Own Brain!

Let's take a grand tour of the brain regions involved in what we're calling "neurological and systemic independence." These aren't official neuroscience terms (you won't find them in a medical textbook between the hippocampus and some mythical "Self-Sufficiency Cortex"), but the mental and emotional skills they describe—like self-awareness, emotional regulation, autonomy, and resilience—are very real and linked to well-studied brain networks. In short, science backs this up, even if it didn't come up with the exact branding.

Now, you don't need a neuroscience degree to benefit from knowing how your brain works. You don't even need to remember the fancy Latin names. But having a basic understanding of what different brain regions do can be surprisingly useful—kind of like knowing where the power switch is before calling tech support. For instance, when you realize that the prefrontal cortex is responsible for rational decision-making, it suddenly makes sense why it takes years to fully develop (explaining many questionable teenage life choices). Or when you learn that the amygdala is involved in emotional responses, you can start to recognize when it's overreacting—like when you feel personally attacked by a slow internet connection.

The point is, your brain has built-in systems that can either work for you or against you, depending on how you engage them. Instead of trying to brute-force your way into better habits or more independence, you can take advantage of how your brain is already wired. Think of it like using a map instead of wandering around hoping you'll eventually stumble upon a sense of clarity. With a little awareness of your own mental machinery, you can train yourself to respond more thoughtfully, regulate emotions more effectively, and build the kind of independence that isn't just wishful thinking—but something grounded in actual brain science. And that beats relying on sheer willpower any day.

Cognitive Limitations: Why Awareness Alone Isn't Enough

While understanding how these brain regions work can be empowering, it's equally important to acknowledge the limitations of the brain, such as biases, cognitive distortions, and unconscious processes.

The Illusion of Control – Your Brain's Prediction Bias: Your brain is wired to predict patterns, often seeing connections that don't exist (a phenomenon known as 'patternicity'). This is why we sometimes may assume someone is upset with us based on a single text or facial expression—our brains fill in missing information with worst-case scenarios. Even with awareness, we still need external feedback, self-reflection, and sometimes professional guidance to override these built-in biases.

Cognitive Load – Why Too Many Decisions Drain Your Brain: Your PFC is powerful, but it has limited bandwidth. This is why decision fatigue happens—after making too many choices in a day, your brain starts defaulting to the easiest or most familiar option, which may not always be the best. This is why many successful people (like Steve Jobs and Barack Obama) simplify decisions like wardrobe choices—they save cognitive energy for more important tasks. To optimize your mental energy, try setting small, automatic habits (e.g., pre-planning meals or morning routines) to streamline unnecessary daily decisions.

By understanding how these different brain regions function—and where they might trip us up—you can train yourself to make better decisions, regulate emotions more effectively, and navigate life with greater independence. The goal isn't perfection, but awareness and small, intentional changes that help you take control of your brain rather than letting it control you.

So the next time your amygdala freaks out over a slow internet connection or your PFC debates buying that impulse gadget, remember—you've got an entire Divine Council in your brain. And with the right awareness, Life Itself can lead them toward more cohesion, peace, and joy.

Meeting Your Inner Divine Council

You come fully equipped to face every obstacle with the full force of your inner council behind you—all working together to help you navigate, adapt, and grow.

Prefrontal Cortex (PFC): your trusted decision-maker — LOGIC

Amygdala: a loyal protector, or a panicked instigator — EMOTION

Anterior Singular Cortex (ACC): your wise mediator — INTUITION

Isula: your silent, grounding body-sensor — AWARENESS

Hippocampus: your tireless, experienced librarian — MEMORY

Default Mode Network (DMN): your baseline of contentment —STATE OF BEING

Before we dive deeper into the science, imagine this while you continue through this chapter:

As mentioned your brain has a lot of parts. Each part has a job, kind of like a team. A weird, wacky, brilliant, chaotic team. And just like any team, each member wants to succeed in their role.

Some parts are cool under pressure. Others hit the panic button a little too fast. Some want to plan everything five years in advance. Others are just waiting to be put in the game when you need them.

Over the next few pages, you'll get to meet them. But first...

Imagine your brain as a team of characters. Maybe ones you can already picture from a movie, show, cartoon or comic. Maybe ones you make up completely from scratch based on what you learn. What would they look like? Sound like? Act like?

Use the space on the next page to jot down some ideas of how you may like to picture the parts of your brain working together.

At the end of each description, use the blank Character Cards to invent your brain's cast as we go. There are no wrong answers—just remember:

Your goal is to understand how these characters interact, how they help, or potentially harm, your daily life, and how you can 'coach' them to work together like the dream team they're meant to be.

Growing Up!

Prefrontal Cortex (PFC): The Wise Decision-Maker

Your prefrontal cortex is the CEO of your brain. It governs rational thought, long-term planning, and impulse control. Without it, you'd be at the mercy of every fleeting emotion or distraction.

Ever felt torn between impulse-buying that expensive gadget and saving money for something more meaningful? That's your prefrontal cortex battling your dopamine-hungry reward system. When you pause before making a purchase and ask, 'Do I really need this, or is this just my brain chasing a quick dopamine hit?'—you're engaging your PFC. Strengthening this part of your brain through mindful decision-making (like taking 24 hours before any big purchase) helps you avoid financial regret and develop better long-term habits.

Research from Stanford University (Bechara et al., 2000) found that individuals with prefrontal cortex damage struggle with long-term decision-making and often make impulsive choices. This highlights why training your PFC through mindfulness and strategic pausing can help strengthen rational thinking, reducing impulsivity and improving life choices.

The PFC Character Card is on the next page. When you think about the traits discussed above, what kind of character comes to mind? Draw and/or describe your character in a way that makes them memorable to you. Remember, you can always come back and add or edit aspects of any of your team members.

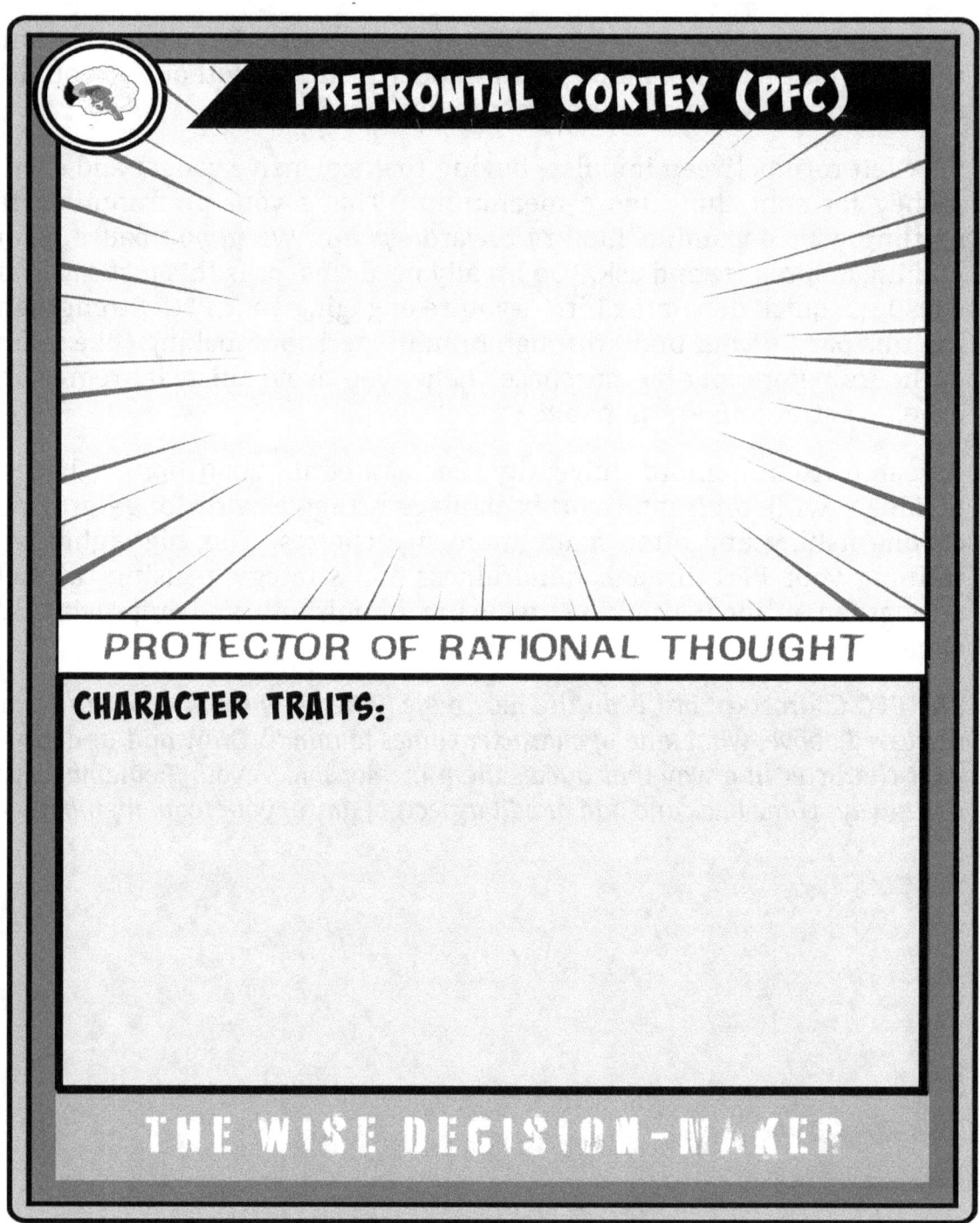

Amygdala: The Emotional Alarm System

The amygdala is like an overzealous security guard. Its job is to detect threats and trigger emotional responses—great for avoiding danger, but not always great for handling everyday stress.

A study by LeDoux (1996) on fear conditioning showed that the amygdala processes emotional threats faster than the PFC, explaining why we react before thinking in stressful situations. This is why deep breathing techniques and grounding exercises help—activating the parasympathetic nervous system counteracts the amygdala's overreaction, restoring balance to emotional regulation.

Imagine you're in a meeting, and your boss unexpectedly asks you a question. Your heart races, your palms sweat, and your mind goes blank. That's your amygdala hijacking your rational brain, throwing you into fight, flight, freeze or follow mode. But if you train yourself to take a slow, deep breath before responding, you engage the prefrontal cortex, which calms the amygdala and helps you think clearly. This simple trick can turn high-pressure moments into opportunities for composed, confident responses.

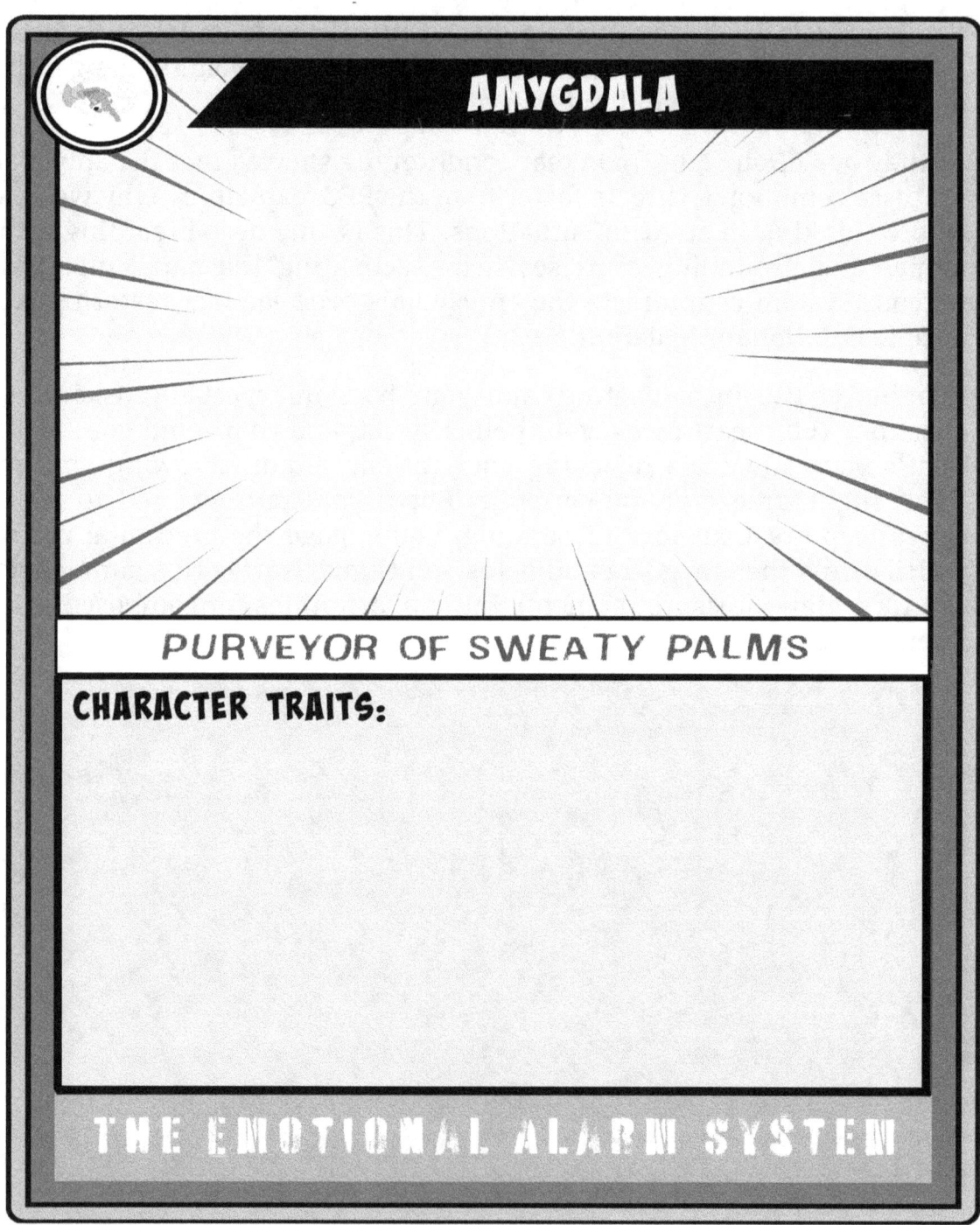

Prefrontal Cortex and Amygdala: Your Brain's Navigation System

Imagine your inner council gathering for a crucial decision. At the head of the table sits the Prefrontal Cortex, the wise and ever-calm council leader, who lays out the plan with the finesse of a seasoned diplomat. It gently advises, "Let's take a deep breath and consider our options before we act"—a friendly reminder not to send that overly dramatic text when emotions are running high.

Sitting nearby is the Amygdala, the council's hyper-alert sentinel, always ready to shout, "Danger! Danger!" at even the slightest hint of trouble. Whether it's a mildly judgmental glance at the grocery store or a shadow that looks suspiciously like a potential threat, the Amygdala is on it like a fire alarm at an indoor barbeque. While its split-second reactions served our ancestors well during encounters with saber-toothed tigers, nowadays they sometimes turn everyday mishaps into a full-blown melodrama.

When these two work in harmony, they strike the perfect balance between thoughtful planning and necessary caution, guiding you smoothly through life's twists and turns with both wisdom and a touch of humor. However, if the overzealous sentinel starts dominating the discussion, decisions can quickly become as dramatic as a soap opera—overreacting to every minor hiccup and throwing your well-planned route off course.

A Day in the Life: When the PFC and Amygdala Don't Get Along

To fully appreciate how these two interact, let's take a look at some common, everyday struggles.

Scenario 1: The Grocery Store Panic

Everything is going fine until—oh no—you accidentally make eye contact with a stranger in the bread aisle.

> **Amygdala:** "OH NO, WE JUST MADE EYE CONTACT. THEY'RE JUDGING US. DANGER! AVOID! RUN!"

PFC: "Relax, it's just another person. A simple nod will do."

Amygdala: "NOPE. INITIATING AWKWARD AVOIDANCE STRATEGY."

PFC: "Hold your neurons... we could just smile like a normal person?"

Amygdala: "TOO LATE. LOOKING DOWN. PRETENDING TO BE FASCINATED BY WHEAT BREAD."

Scenario 2: The Email Incident

You suddenly remember an email you forgot to respond to... two weeks ago.

Amygdala: "WE FORGOT TO REPLY! WE'RE GOING TO GET FIRED!"

PFC: "It's Sunday at 10 PM. No one is checking emails right now."

Amygdala: "MUST APOLOGIZE IMMEDIATELY. WRITE A LONG EMAIL SAYING WE ARE TERRIBLE. USE LOTS OF EXCLAMATION MARKS!!!"

PFC: "Maybe let's draft something a little more... reasonable?"

Amygdala: "FINE, BUT CC EVERYONE JUST IN CASE."

This push-and-pull is happening constantly, sometimes over big decisions, sometimes over completely irrational fears. For most people, this internal struggle is just an occasional inconvenience. But for individuals with Executive Function Disorder (EFD), it's not just an occasional debate—it's the default setting.

"How does this look for me? Do those examples resemble my inner dialogues?" In the space below, reflect on some of the situations you've experienced that caused mixed feelings or panic. Which parts of the brain were sending which thoughts? Draw or discuss, with the help of the characters you created before, how the interaction may have looked, and how you might have wanted those characters to act to make the situation go more smoothly.

Why Strengthening the PFC is Extra Important for People with EFD

For individuals with EFD, the brain's navigation system has a few extra "spices." The PFC, which normally helps with planning, impulse control, and emotional regulation, sometimes feels like it's on an extended coffee break, leaving the Amygdala in charge way too often. This can make life feel like trying to drive through an unfamiliar city without a working GPS—where every wrong turn feels catastrophic, and distractions pull you in every direction. Tasks that seem routine to others, like organizing a to-do list or remembering to reply to a message, can become overwhelming without strong executive functioning skills. And when the PFC struggles to step in, guess what happens? The Amygdala takes over—treating minor mistakes as high-stakes emergencies.

This is why strengthening the PFC is a game-changer for people with EFD. The good news? The brain has something called neuroplasticity, meaning the PFC can be trained and strengthened over time with intentional strategies like mindfulness, structured routines, and cognitive training. The stronger the PFC, the better it can pause before reacting, prioritize tasks without getting overwhelmed, and regulate emotions without spiraling. Essentially, it upgrades your brain's navigation system from "random panic mode" to "thoughtful decision-making."

The Hidden Advantages of EFD

But let's not forget something important: having EFD isn't just about challenges—it comes with some serious strengths too. A less rigid executive function system often means people with EFD are highly creative, adaptable, and exceptional problem solvers. While neurotypical brains might stick to conventional paths, EFD brains tend to see connections others miss, making them great at thinking outside the box, innovating, and handling unexpected situations with humor and flexibility.

The goal of developing the PFC isn't to suppress these strengths—it's to refine them. A strong PFC allows people with EFD to turn their creativity into action, ensuring that great ideas don't just stay ideas but actually get executed. It also helps with emotional regulation, keeping stress and impulsivity from interfering with their talents. Instead of seeing executive function challenges as a limitation, they can be reframed as a unique cognitive style that, when properly supported, allows for both flexibility and focus. In short, people with EFD aren't just "managing" their brains—they're optimizing them in ways that can make them even more dynamic and capable than their neurotypical peers.

Final Thoughts: Mastering the Balance

At the end of the day, neurological and systemic independence isn't about shutting down the Amygdala or turning the PFC into a strict, joyless taskmaster—it's about balance. Your brain's navigation system works best when logic and emotion work together, giving you the ability to pause, think, and choose how to respond rather than just reacting on autopilot.

For some people, this balance comes naturally. For others—especially those with EFD—it's a skill that has to be consciously developed. But the good news? It can be developed. And once it is, it's a superpower that lets you take control of your own mind, make confident decisions, and navigate life on your own terms. No unnecessary panic required.

What are some traits of your own brain that you consider strengths? How do you use them to your advantage? Do they ever become weaknesses?

Anterior Cingulate Cortex (ACC): The Wise Bridge Keeper of the Mind

The ACC acts like a bridge between the PFC and the amygdala, helping balance logical decision-making and emotional responses. It's crucial for self-awareness and emotional regulation. Imagine the ACC as being the most perfect parents that helps resolve sibling conflict in the most loving, thoughtful and educational ways. When this part of your inner council is allowed to govern the team, all parts of the brain start to understand how to be part of a happy and functional family. You start to feel the power of being able to parent the parts of yourself that might not have been attended to by your parents of origin. You no longer have to hold your parents in contempt and can finally grow up into your own powerful navigator of Life Itself.

Ever had an argument where you regretted what you said moments later? That's your amygdala reacting before your ACC can mediate. The next time someone upsets you, try counting to five before responding. This brief pause gives your ACC time to engage, allowing you to choose words that reflect your true intent rather than reacting impulsively. Strengthening this brain region through practices like mindfulness and journaling can transform communication in your relationships.

A study by Hölzel et al. (2011) in Psychiatry Research found that meditators had increased gray matter density in the anterior cingulate cortex (ACC), improving emotional regulation and self-awareness. This means simple mindfulness exercises—like daily breathwork or body scans—can physically reshape the brain for better resilience and emotional balance.

Even when the council's assembly grows restless—with emotions surging like an impassioned chorus or logic attempting to rush ahead—the ACC ensures that every voice is harmonized, and no decision is made in haste. It's quiet humor and unwavering wisdom remind the inner divine council that balance is the key to navigating life's myriad challenges. In this way, the ACC not only maintains order in your Inner Council mansion, but also infuses the council with a sense of serenity and grace, allowing your inner wisdom to shine through in every decision. With a tender smile and a calm, measured tone, the ACC gently advises, "Let us take a moment to reflect before moving forward."

A Tale of Two Lands

On one side of the bridge lies Emotion Valley where the amygdala presides, a land of rolling storms, golden sunrises, and dramatic monologues. This is where the poets, artists, and fiery rebels of your mind dwell, sending messengers across the bridge with urgent declarations like:

> "This is an emotional emergency! We must react NOW!"

> "We should definitely cry about this for three hours!"

> "Or maybe express our feelings… through interpretive dance?"

On the other side stands Logic City where the PFC presides, a land of perfectly structured buildings, meticulous spreadsheets, and strict zoning laws. Its residents—the strategists, planners, and inner bureaucrats—march to the bridge with neat scrolls reading:

> "Before we panic, let's conduct a cost-benefit analysis."

> "We should consider all possible outcomes before making a decision."

> "Is this even a logical response? Let's create a ten-step plan first."

And in between them, the bridge keeper (ACC) watches it all unfold, weighing emotions against reason, deciding when to let feelings through and when to tell Logic City to take a chill pill.

When the Bridge Becomes Chaos

On most days, the ACC does its job well, maintaining harmony. But when things go sideways—like when both Emotion Valley and Logic City storm the bridge at the same time—the bridge keeper mutters:

> "Oh no. Here we go again."

> "EVERYBODY, JUST BREATHE."

> "I need a raise."

Without the ACC, Logic City would become a soulless bureaucracy, and Emotion Valley would dissolve into endless chaos. But with its guidance, your mind navigates life with both wisdom and warmth, allowing you to respond to situations rather than just react.

Why It Matters

A strong ACC helps you recognize when you're being pulled by external pressures (systemic) or caught in habitual thoughts (neurological). Increased ACC activity is linked to emotional resilience, cognitive flexibility, and better decision-making—allowing you to be both thoughtful and intuitive, without getting stuck in overthinking or overreacting.

In short, strengthening your ACC is like letting your divine parents do their job and the children get to be at home where they don't get overwhelmed, burnt out, or tempted to just abandon the mansion altogether. And with the right tools—mindfulness, cognitive training, and self-awareness—you can help them become a true master of the crossroads.

Once again, how can you relate to these examples? Think of a situation where the bridge became chaos in your mind? Use the space below to draw a comic strip or write a skit about how your Inner Coucil worked together, or against each other.

Interoception and the Insula

Interoception is the silent symphony of the self, the music of being played within the temple of the body.

It is the hidden orchestra whose melodies we do not consciously compose, yet whose harmonies shape our every moment. The heartbeat drums its steady rhythm, the breath hums through the wind instruments of the lungs, and the gut plucks the deep strings of intuition, resonating with truths we feel before we understand. The skin plays its subtle harp, responding to warmth and chill, while the muscles provide the bassline of tension and release.

But who listens to this music?

A mind untuned to interoception is like a person rushing through life with noise-canceling headphones—oblivious to the wisdom humming within. Yet, the adept, the philosopher, the seeker—they learn to hear.

To them, interoception is the inner concert hall where self-awareness unfolds, where the body and soul meet in whispered dialogue. Hunger is not just an urge—it is the low, yearning notes of a cello. Fatigue is not just a burden—it is the slow decrescendo of an overplayed violin. Peace is not just a thought—it is the quiet resonance of a well-tuned instrument in harmony with existence.

The insula, then, is the composer's hand, conducting the nonverbal flow of sensation into the symphony of self-awareness. It decides which notes rise to attention and which fade into the background, ensuring we are neither overwhelmed by sensation nor deaf to the whispers of our own being.

To cultivate interoception is to learn to listen—to recognize that the body is not a separate machine but an instrument of consciousness, constantly singing, humming, and breathing its truth. The wise do not merely hear this music; they learn to play along.

If interoception is the musician of the soul, then the insula is its sound engineer, the behind-the-scenes genius in the recording studio of the mind, fine-tuning the grand symphony of bodily awareness so that we neither become hyper-focused on the feeling of our own socks or the tag on our shirt, nor completely forget we need food until we're irrationally angry.

Picture it: the body is a vast orchestra, each section playing a different sensation. The heartbeat provides the steady percussion, the breath swells and falls like a cello, and the stomach contributes an occasional dramatic drumroll when it's time to eat. The skin plays a subtle harp melody of warmth and coolness, while the muscles hum a low bassline of tension and relaxation. Even pain has its own section—a blaring trumpet if you stub your toe, or an ominous string tremor when you sense illness creeping in.

But if all these sensations blasted at full volume, it would be chaos. This is where the insula steps in, adjusting the levels, deciding what gets turned up and what fades into background noise. You don't need a full orchestra reminding you that your shirt is touching your skin every second of the day, but you do need an urgent cymbal crash when you've accidentally placed your hand on a hot stove.

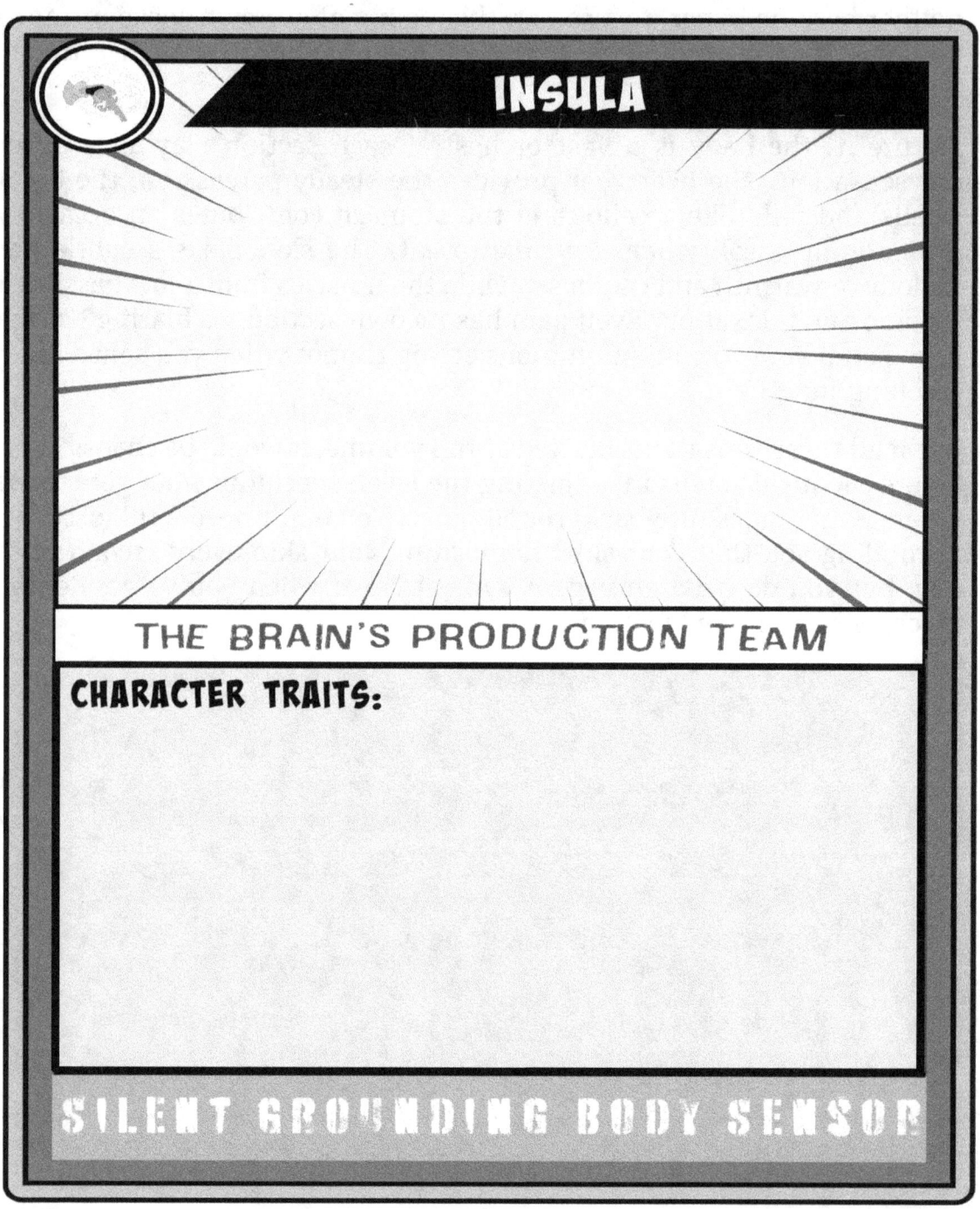

The Insula's Struggles: Managing Surprise Guest Performances

- But the insula's job isn't just about keeping everything in harmony. It also has to deal with surprise guest musicians crashing the stage.

- Stress bursts in with an impromptu electric guitar solo, throwing off the entire tempo.

- Anxiety hijacks the percussion section, turning your heartbeat into an unpredictable drumroll.

- Nostalgia sneaks in like a wistful violin solo, triggered by the smell of cookies from childhood.

- Love? That's when the insula turns up the strings, creating a sweeping cinematic score every time you see that person.

- Gut feelings? The insula gets a memo from the subconscious saying, "Cue the suspenseful soundtrack, something's off."

And let's not forget those awkward moments when the insula tries to send an important warning, but the brain refuses to listen.

- Insula: "Hey, we're really dehydrated. Maybe drink some water?"

- Brain: "Or... hear me out... another coffee."

- Insula: "...Fine, but don't blame me when your hands start shaking like a jazz drummer on espresso."

Or the classic:

- Gut: "I have a bad feeling about this."

- Brain: "Pffft. It'll be fine."

- Ten minutes later... disaster.

When the Insula Is Overworked: A Musical Mess

When the insula struggles, the whole symphony goes haywire. Ever had those moments where you suddenly become too aware of your own breathing? Or your heartbeat feels weirdly noticeable for no reason? That's the insula turning the wrong knobs, making background sensations way too loud.

On the flip side, when it's underactive, you might forget to notice pain or exhaustion until it's too late—like realizing you've been sitting awkwardly for hours and now your leg has gone completely numb.

And of course, when we're sleep-deprived, the insula just gives up entirely. Now everything is either muted beyond recognition or painfully amplified. Your emotions swing wildly like a jazz improv gone wrong, and your body feels like a badly tuned orchestra held together with duct tape and sheer willpower.

A Masterpiece in the Making

Despite all the chaos, the insula never stops working, tirelessly fine-tuning the music of self-awareness. It is the unseen conductor of your internal orchestra, ensuring that every bodily sensation, every flicker of emotion, and every whisper of intuition finds its place in the grand symphony of existence. Without it, interoception would be a cacophony—a band without a conductor, where hunger drums too loudly, anxiety plays an unscheduled solo, and exhaustion tries to pass off as motivation. We'd struggle to distinguish between genuine physiological needs and fleeting emotional impulses, mistaking thirst for stress, fatigue for sadness, or boredom for hunger.

But with the insula in charge, our internal awareness becomes a beautifully orchestrated masterpiece. On good days, it's a graceful waltz of homeostasis, every instrument in perfect sync, playing a melody of balance and well-being. On stressful days, it can feel like an intense rock ballad, heart pounding like a drum, cortisol shredding on lead guitar. And of course, when we're running on three hours of sleep and sheer determination, it occasionally descends into a slightly out-of-tune kazoo solo, where everything feels just a little off, but somehow, we're still moving forward.

By tuning into the body's signals, we foster deeper self-awareness and gain the ability to respond rather than react. A well-functioning insula helps us navigate stress and social pressures with greater resilience. It sharpens emotional intelligence, allowing us to interpret feelings more accurately—not just in others, but in ourselves. This includes self-empathy, the gentle art of acknowledging our own needs and limits, rather than ignoring them in the name of productivity or external expectations.

In the grand composition of the mind, the insula doesn't seek the spotlight, yet without it, the music of our inner world would be lost in disarray.

Can you see the different characteristics and, in our case, characters of the brain coming together? How do you see the insula working with the members of your brain's devine council you've developed so far? Can you picture, or even feel examples in the real world in which all of these parts were contributing to your thoughts or decision making processes?

Hippocampus: The Keeper of Memory—Librarian, Lighthouse, and Storyteller

The hippocampus is the tireless librarian of your mind's grand library—slightly overworked, occasionally frazzled, but endlessly dedicated to keeping your memories in order. Day in and day out, it scurries through endless aisles of experience, plucking the right books off the shelves when you need to recall where you left your keys, the name of that person you just met, or the lyrics to a song you haven't heard in years. Of course, like any librarian managing an ever-expanding collection, it sometimes fumbles—handing you a completely unrelated book when you ask for the right one, leaving you awkwardly greeting an old friend with the wrong name or walking into a room only to forget why you're there in the first place.

But beyond its daily duties, the hippocampus is also the lighthouse of your inner ocean, casting steady beams of remembrance across the rolling waves of time. When life's tides pull you away, it signals you back to shore, illuminating the moments that shape your story. It safeguards the continuity of your identity, ensuring that the person you were yesterday is meaningfully connected to the person you are today. Like an old storyteller by the fire, it collects the whispers of the past and threads them into the fabric of the present, weaving the narrative of your life with care and precision.

Of course, even the most diligent librarian or lighthouse keeper needs a break. Sometimes, it misplaces a name, files a memory in the wrong section, or momentarily leaves you stranded in a sea of forgetfulness. But it's doing its best—after all, keeping track of a lifetime's worth of memories is no small task!

The hippocampus plays a crucial role in memory formation and retrieval, serving as both the architect and guardian of experience. Beyond memory, it also contributes to stress resilience and emotional regulation, helping us process and integrate life's challenges.

Chronic stress, trauma, or overwhelming social pressure can shrink the hippocampus over time, as seen in conditions like major depression and

PTSD. However, just as a well-kept library expands and a lighthouse stands firm against the storm, the hippocampus can be nurtured and strengthened. Practices like meditation, reflection, and conscious stress management—essential for both systemic and neurological independence—can help maintain or even increase its volume, ensuring that the guiding light of memory continues to shine across the vast ocean of the self.

Enjoy working on the hippocampus character card on the next page. It's always one of my favorites.

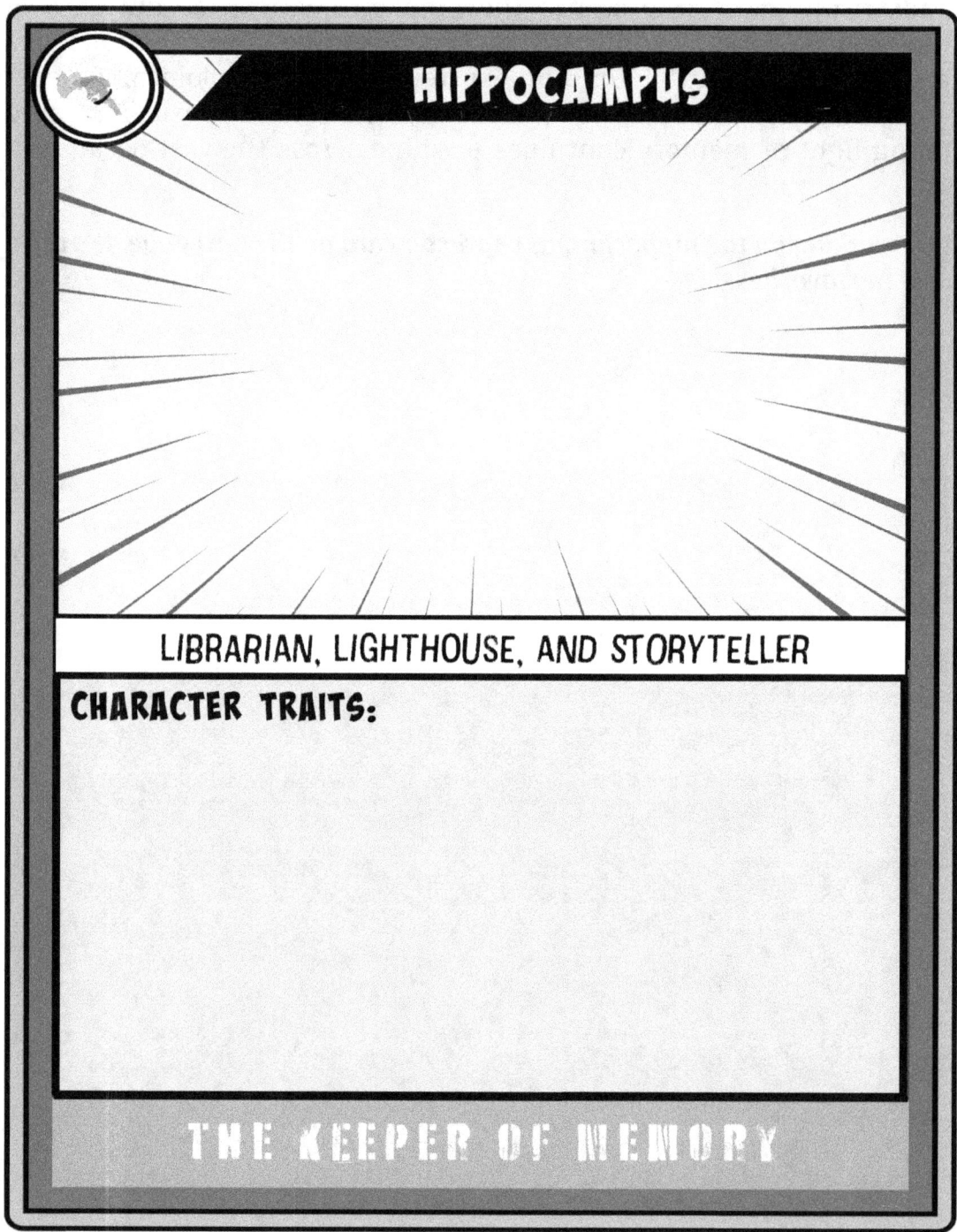

I have included a very sweet letter from the mother of your hippocampus. After all, mother knows best!

My Dearest Hippocampus,

Sweetheart, you must start taking better care of yourself. I see you running around like a frazzled little librarian, trying to keep track of a lifetime's worth of memories, and honestly, it's exhausting just watching you. You work so hard, but you forget the most important thing—you need to take care of yourself, too. So sit down, take a deep breath, and let your loving mother give you some advice.

First of all, you need to write things down. I know you think you can remember everything, but let's be honest—you've already mixed up names, misplaced countless keys, and walked into a room with absolutely no idea why you're there. Keep a journal, tell stories, talk to a friend—just do something to help yourself out. I can't keep bailing you out every time you blank on someone's birthday.

And while we're at it, keep learning new things! You're so smart, but if you don't challenge yourself, you'll just end up replaying the same old memories like a greatest hits album from 10 years ago. Take up a new hobby, read a book, or, I don't know, finally learn how to play that instrument you swore you'd master. Your neurons crave new experiences—feed them!

Speaking of new experiences, go outside once in a while. You love exploring new places! It keeps you sharp! Take a different route home, wander through an unfamiliar part of town, go on a little adventure. The more you navigate new spaces, the stronger you become. I know you love to be a homebody sometimes, but let's not turn you into a hermit, okay?

Now, this one is important, so listen closely—stop stressing yourself out! I mean it. If you keep letting stress run your life, you're going to shrink. No, really, stress actually makes you smaller, and I did not raise you to let yourself waste away like that. Meditation, deep breathing, journaling—do something to calm yourself down. And no, overthinking everything at 3 AM does not count as "problem-solving."

While we're on the topic of health, you need to exercise. You don't have to run a marathon, but for goodness' sake, move your body! You love being active—dancing, walking, swimming—it helps you grow new brain cells, which, trust me, you need. The last thing you want is to start misfiling memories because you got too lazy to stretch those neurons.

And for the love of all things good, get some sleep! You think you're fine on five hours? You're not. Do you want to be wandering around in a daze, forgetting why you opened the fridge? No? Then get your rest. Your memories depend on it, and frankly, so does your dignity.

Lastly, have some fun, my love. You work so hard, and I appreciate everything you do, but if you don't take time to enjoy life, what's the point? Listen to music, laugh until your sides hurt, create something beautiful, or just spend time with people who make you happy. Laughter and joy keep you strong, and you deserve that.

So, my darling hippocampus, take care of yourself. You're the lighthouse of the mind, the guardian of stories, the reason we all know who we are. But even the wisest librarians and the brightest lighthouses need maintenance. Eat well, rest, and please—stop stressing so much. You'll thank me later.

With all my love,

Your Ever-Vigilant (But Very Proud) Mother

Do you like mom's advice? Anything you would add or change? Do you feel like you should sketch out an image of your hippocampus's mother?

Default Mode Network (DMN)

The Default Mode Network (DMN) is a network of brain regions that becomes active when the mind is at rest, particularly during introspection, daydreaming, self-reflection, and recalling past experiences. Often referred to as the brain's "background mode," the DMN plays a critical role in self-awareness, identity, social cognition, and mental time travel—the ability to relive past events or imagine future scenarios. This network consists of several interconnected brain regions, including the medial prefrontal cortex (mPFC), which is involved in self-referential thinking and decision-making, and the posterior cingulate cortex (PCC) and precuneus, which support autobiographical memory, consciousness, and the integration of self-related thoughts. The inferior parietal lobule (IPL) contributes to perspective-taking and social cognition, while the hippocampus facilitates memory recall and the simulation of possible future experiences. The lateral temporal cortex assists in processing and interpreting social narratives.

Functionally, the DMN serves as the brain's internal reflection system, fostering self-awareness and constructing a continuous sense of identity. It is also responsible for spontaneous thoughts, creativity, and problem-solving. Additionally, it enables social cognition, allowing individuals to understand and anticipate others' emotions and perspectives. The DMN constructs the narrative of one's life through autobiographical thinking, linking past experiences to the present and future. In short, this is your global state of being.

Dysregulation of the DMN is associated with mental health challenges. An overactive DMN can lead to excessive rumination, anxiety, and depression, as the brain becomes trapped in negative self-reflective loops. Conversely, an underactive DMN can result in difficulties with self-awareness and identity, often observed in disorders such as ADHD and dissociative conditions. Practices like meditation and mindfulness help regulate the DMN, fostering a balance between self-reflection and present-moment awareness. This network, though often operating in the background, plays a crucial role in shaping an individual's inner world, guiding self-perception, memory, and imagination.

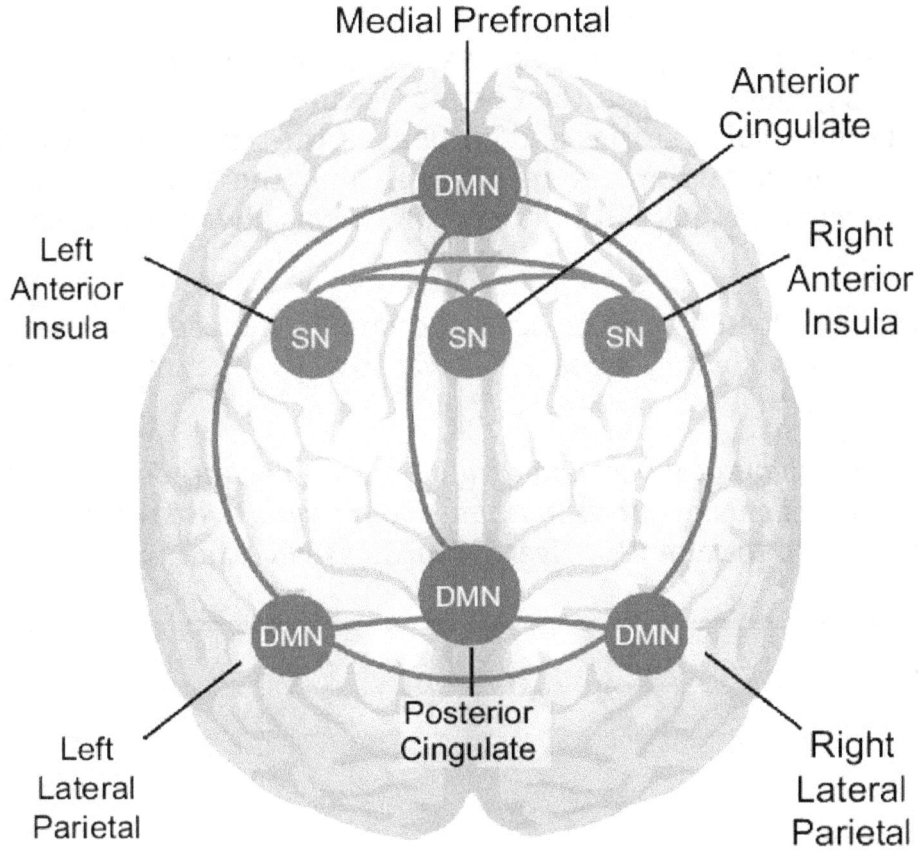

The Inner River and the Cosmic Ocean

Imagine your mind as a vast and winding river, shaped by time and experience. This Inner River of Echoes flows ceaselessly, carrying memories, identities, and the silent narratives that define your sense of self. It whispers of separateness, of boundaries—of "you" as distinct from the world around you.

But in moments of deep stillness—through meditation, surrender, or profound awareness—the river slows. The currents settle, the ripples of thought fade, and something vast shimmers beneath the surface. The river, once so certain of its course, begins to recognize a deeper truth: it was never separate from the ocean. The very water that defined its journey was always moving toward reunion.

As the river surrenders, its edges dissolve. Its waters spill beyond the familiar banks, merging with the Cosmic Ocean—a boundless, infinite expanse where personal stories and burdens of the past and future dissolve. There is no judgment here, no resistance—only the quiet recognition that the river was never apart from the ocean. It was always the ocean in motion.

Yet, nothing is lost. The river does not vanish; instead, it remembers. It was never just a solitary stream—it was always an expression of something infinite.

Draw or write about your vast and winding river. What are some of the echoes, memories, and silent narratives that cause your river's twists, turns, and rapids? How do you plan to calm your river? What steps will you take to make it truly shimmer?

The Default Mode Network: When the Inner River Quietens

This is what happens when the Default Mode Network (DMN) quiets. The habitual self-referencing, the constant narration of identity, the illusion of separateness—they all begin to fade. And in their place, there is only vastness. Awareness. Pure presence. The moment where the drop remembers it was always the sea.

But the DMN does not merely "turn off"—it transforms. The mind does not become empty; it becomes vast.

From River to Radiance: A Cosmic Perspective

Rather than dissolving into nothingness, the mind expands into everythingness. Imagine the brain not just as a river flowing toward dissolution but as a luminous galactic nexus—its neural pathways woven from stardust, connected by cosmic filaments. The radiant core at its center represents deep awareness: the moment when self-referential thought collapses, and pure presence takes over.

You are not just the river.

You are not just the ocean.

You are both.

Now that you've created your divine council, how do you see each of the characters coming together to help you expand your brain and help take it from rough river to a galaxy of endless light and opportunity? What does it look like if all members of the council work together in perfect harmony?

Primary Nodes: The Core Modules of Your Divine Code

Imagine your inner Divine Council—the sacred assembly within you—being constantly upheld and fine-tuned by an elite team of master programmers, tirelessly maintaining the intricate operating system of your being. These masterful architects of your inner world ensure that every line of code functions with precision, keeping your system in harmony, efficiency, and peak performance.

At the core of this divine architecture are the Primary Nodes, each acting as an essential module within your system's master code. These nodes are the central processing units that regulate the intricate balance between logic, emotion, intuition, and awareness. When one of these modules experiences a disruption—be it due to emotional turbulence, mental exhaustion, or external chaos—it's akin to a critical system error, a glitch that slows down, distorts, or even crashes the entire program of your existence.

Ancient wisdom has long recognized these energy centers as chakras, powerful hubs of consciousness that govern the flow of life-force energy. However, modern Western thought—often reluctant to acknowledge the vast, timeless knowledge that predates the Renaissance—labels them as mere nodes, stripping them of their profound spiritual essence. This reluctance to accept that ancient civilizations had access to deep, universal truths is an unfortunate limitation, but one that does not diminish the power of these energy centers. That discussion, however, belongs in another book.

What truly matters here is understanding how these core modules function within your divine code—how each Primary Node plays a pivotal role in your overall balance, cognition, and spiritual vitality. To master your system is to become the conscious programmer of your own being, fine-tuning your internal code so that your Divine Council can operate in its fullest glory. But these nodes don't just help you manage your own experiences—they provide access to universal intelligence that extends beyond personal memory, history, or experience. They function as antennas, receivers, and processors, granting you the ability to download wisdom from the vast network of existence itself.

You see, these nodes are like transducers in a radio, designed to receive and decode information from vast, unseen frequencies of existence. Just as radio waves are constantly surrounding us—imperceptible until we use a receiver to tune into the right frequency—the brain's Default Mode Network (DMN) when it is in its expansive state, and its Primary Nodes function as intricate receivers, picking up and interpreting the deeper wavelengths of thought, intuition, and universal intelligence. We may not see the signals of knowledge and insight floating around us, but they are always there, waiting to be accessed. When a transducer is finely tuned to the right station, voilà, music flows through, filling the silence with harmony and meaning. Likewise, when your internal transducers—your DMN nodes—are aligned and sensitive, they allow you to access hidden depths of awareness, creative inspiration, and even knowledge that seems to come from beyond personal memory or direct experience. This is precisely how we change our state of being toward whatever you are hoping to create in your world.

Wavelengths of information exist in unseen formats, spanning the past, present, and even possible futures. Every thought, emotion, and idea carries a frequency, and by fine-tuning these nodes, your Divine Council can tap into different layers of reality—deciphering wisdom that is not just personal but collective, ancestral, and even cosmic in origin. The more sensitive and refined the transducer, the greater the range of frequencies you can receive. This means that a well-calibrated DMN doesn't just help you process memories or daydream—it grants you access to higher cognition, deeper intuition, and expansive creativity. It allows your Prefrontal Cortex (PFC), Hippocampus, and Anterior Cingulate Cortex (ACC) to work in harmony, unlocking profound insights, visionary ideas, and moments of genius that seem to emerge from nowhere.

However, just as a poorly tuned radio struggles with static, distortion, or missed signals, an unbalanced DMN can disrupt your connection to these higher frequencies. If too sensitive, it may pick up excessive noise—leading to overthinking, anxiety, or intrusive thoughts that cloud clarity. If too weak, it may fail to capture meaningful insights, resulting in mental fog, forgetfulness, and a loss of connection to deeper awareness.

The key is refinement, learning how to adjust your internal tuning so that the Divine Council receives the clearest, most meaningful transmissions. Through practices like meditation, self-reflection, deep focus, and mindfulness, you sharpen your transducer, expanding the number of channels you can access. The more attuned you become, the richer the symphony of wisdom, creativity, and insight that flows through you—an orchestra of intelligence playing on the wavelengths of existence itself.

Thoughts?

Root Node: The Power Supply Module—Grounding into the Collective Foundation

This is the foundational code that initializes your entire system. Think of it as the power supply that ensures your hardware is properly grounded and ready to run. It connects you to the ancestral archives of human survival, instinct, and primal knowing—a database encoded into the very fabric of life. This node remembers truths beyond your personal experience—it stores the instincts that guide you in times of crisis, the deep-seeded wisdom passed down through the ages. If this module isn't functioning correctly, you may feel disconnected, unsafe, or unworthy, like a device with no reliable power source. In your physical body, this node is located at the very tail of your spine. If you've ever fallen on your tail bone and received an enormous surge of electricity that goes up your spine, you might have felt the power of the root node.

When you think of the sources of energy within your body, what comes to mind? When could you try and consiously access your Root Node?

Sacral Node: The Multimedia Streaming Engine—Accessing Creative Flow Beyond Time

This module handles the rich media of your inner experience—emotions, pleasure, and creativity. But creativity is not confined to personal experience. The Sacral Node is like a cosmic file-sharing system, where you can stream inspiration from the collective consciousness. Artists, musicians, and visionaries often describe moments where ideas seem to "come from nowhere"—this is their Sacral Node tapping into a universal creative current. When this node is blocked, inspiration buffers endlessly, passions stall, and you may feel like you've lost your connection to the grand, infinite archive of artistic and emotional expression. In your physical body, this is located just below your naval.

Take note of your thoughts on your Sacral Node.

Solar Plexus Node: The Router of Self-Esteem—Connecting You to the Frequencies of Power

This is your system's personal power router, distributing confidence, willpower, and energy. But confidence is not just a personal trait—it is a frequency, an energetic signature that resonates through time and space. When fully activated, this node allows you to access the certainty and courage of all those who have stood in their power before you—great leaders, warriors, and change-makers who left their mark on history. Their essence is encoded in the collective field, and when your Solar Plexus is tuned properly, you tap into that power. A weakened signal leaves you scrambling for external validation, like a weak Wi-Fi connection desperately trying to reconnect. In your physical body this is located in your upper abdomen just below your diaphragm.

Heart Node: The Social Interface Controller—Linking into the Universal Network of Love

Imagine this module as the customer support gateway to love and connection. The Heart Node is more than just your personal emotional center—it's an interdimensional network linking you to the experiences of every being that has ever loved, grieved, or sought connection. Love transcends time, space, and individual history. This node allows you to access the wisdom of the sages, the kindness of healers, and the compassion of those who have walked before you. When in balance, you can give and receive love without fear or limitation. A blocked module, however, results in emotional disconnection—like being locked out of your account, unable to retrieve the access codes to joy and unity. In your physical body this is located in the center of your chest next you your heart.

Throat Node: The Communication Protocol—Tuning into the Cosmic Broadcast

This core module is your system's microphone and speaker setup, enabling clear, effective self-expression. However, it also functions as an antenna, allowing you to receive wisdom that has never been spoken to you directly. Ever had words flow through you effortlessly, almost as if something greater was speaking through you? That's the Throat Node downloading insights from the collective consciousness. Poets, orators, and truth-speakers often access this stream. When balanced, your words carry resonance and power. If blocked, you may feel muted, unheard, or as though your voice does not matter. In your physical body, this is located in your throat.

Third Eye Node: The Search Engine of Insight—Downloading Universal Intelligence

Serving as your internal Google, this module provides instant clarity and profound insights. But it's not just limited to your personal knowledge base—it pulls from the quantum field of information itself. A fully activated Third Eye means you can access truths you have never learned in conventional ways, almost like a universal AI predicting the answers before you even finish typing the question. Many call this intuition, but in reality, it is your direct connection to cosmic intelligence. A foggy Third Eye leaves you stuck in a cluttered mental database, unable to distinguish profound truth from background noise. In your physical body this is located in the middle of your forehead.

Crown Node: The Satellite Uplink to the Divine—Your Direct Connection to the Infinite Source

This is your system's ultimate connection to higher code—the direct uplink to universal intelligence, divine guidance, and higher frequencies of being. When the Crown Node is active, your entire system is synchronized with the great cosmic blueprint. You receive downloads of wisdom that go beyond words, logic, history, and personal memory. This is where enlightenment happens, where you remember that you are not just a single entity, but an integral part of the vast intelligence of the universe. If it malfunctions, you are left disconnected, buffering endlessly in the search for meaning. This is a node that physically exists a couple inches above the crown of your skull.

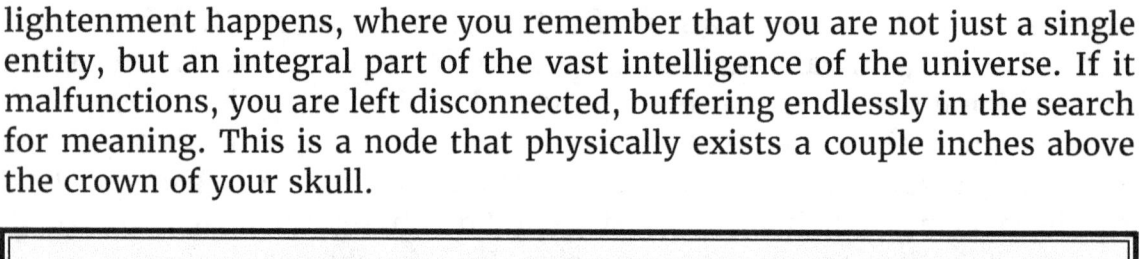

Your Nodes: Access Points to the Universe

These nodes are not just mechanisms for personal awareness—they are gateways to the infinite knowledge of existence. Through them, you have access to the thoughts of the ancients, the wisdom of the ages, the unspoken language of intuition, and the limitless creativity of the cosmos. When properly tuned, your entire being becomes a vessel for divine intelligence, receiving and transmitting frequencies that go beyond the limitations of personal experience.

To master these nodes is to transcend the boundaries of individual perception and step into the universal stream of consciousness itself. You are not just running a program—you are becoming the architect of your own divine operating system.

And here is where the magic truly unfolds—when you meditate or practice mindfulness, you step beyond the limits of your conditioned mind and enter a state of being nothing. And oh, what an electrifying, limitless space that is! In this state, you are not your name, not your past, not your fears, not your programming—you become pure, open-source consciousness, free from the rigid architecture of identity and societal conditioning. You unshackle yourself from the constraints of past experiences, outdated beliefs, and inherited narratives, stepping into the vast expanse where true intelligence flows freely.

This is starting to really sound like true Systemic and Neurological Independence, eh?

This is where Life Itself has full access to you, unobstructed by the mental firewalls of doubt, fear, and illusion. Like a perfectly optimized system, you become receptive to the highest, most refined code—wisdom that is in complete alignment with your true, expansive self, which has never been separate from the cosmos. In this state, you no longer function as a pre-programmed entity running on external scripts—instead, you become the conscious architect of your own reality.

This is systemic and neurological independence in its highest form. No longer are you a passive player, reacting to the circumstances dictated by old paradigms. You step onto the real gameboard of life, where the rules are no longer imposed upon you but created by you. The neural pathways of your brain, once dictated by past conditioning, now fire in alignment with cosmic intelligence rather than unconscious programming. You are no longer trapped in survival mode—you are thriving in creation mode which is your birthright.

Here, in the sacred space of nothingness, the limitations of the material realm dissolve. No longer bound by the outdated laws that once governed your reality, you gain access to the infinite possibilities encoded in existence itself. You realize that you are not just playing the game—you are designing it. You can become anything, because you are no longer running on scripts written by a world that once tried to confine you. You are writing your own divine code—an ever-expanding masterpiece, sourced directly from the infinite intelligence of Life Itself. I vote for this way of navigating this world.

Can you see it all coming together? Are you excited about how systemic and neurological independence working for you?

Training and Sensitizing Your Nodes.

1. Mindfulness Meditation: Taming the Chaos One Breath at a Time

Picture your Prefrontal Cortex (PFC) has grown into wise old sage, patiently waiting for you to stop doom scrolling and just breathe. Meanwhile, your Amygdala—with its fiery tendencies—screams, "We're under attack!" at the sight of an unread email.

Good news: Just 10-15 minutes of meditation a day has been shown (by those super-smart folks at Harvard and UCLA) to actually reshape these brain regions. YOU ARE RESHAPING THESE REGIONS! Not your therapist, not the medications, not the media, YOU! The PFC gets stronger, the Amygdala chills out, and the Anterior Cingulate Cortex (ACC) gets better at balancing logic and emotions and reparenting you perfectly.

Bad news: Your brain will absolutely resist at first. The first few sessions might feel like you're herding cats in a thunderstorm. But keep at it! Your future self—who doesn't panic over a typo in an important email—will thank you.

Make a plan now. When can you set aside 10-15 minutes and start your training? How will it look? What do you need to ensure it happens?

2. Body Scan & Interoceptive Awareness: Becoming Sherlock Holmes of Your Own Body

Your Insula (a brain region responsible for bodily awareness) loves it when you check in on your body. But let's be honest—most of us only notice our bodies when our back suddenly decides to feel 90 years old after sitting for too long or our stomach makes whale noises in a dead-silent meeting.

A body scan meditation helps train your brain to notice tension before it becomes pain and subtle emotional shifts before they turn into full-blown stress meltdowns. Just pause, scan from head to toe, and observe without judgment—like a scientist studying an exotic creature (which, let's face it, we kind of are).

Think of all the times you could check in with your body throughout the day. How might it help you feel better?

3. Cognitive Reappraisal Techniques: Tricking Your Brain into Chill Mode

Ever had a friend dramatically declare, "My life is over!" because their phone battery died? That's an amygdala-driven reaction. Cognitive Reappraisal—used in Cognitive Behavioral Therapy (CBT)—teaches the PFC to step in and say, "Or... we could just find a charger?"

Reframing negative thoughts helps you reinterpret stressful situations. Instead of "I failed that test, I'm doomed," try "I learned what to improve for next time." It's not about lying to yourself—it's about training your brain to look at reality without unnecessary emotional explosions.

Bonus: This also makes you way more fun to be around. Your friends will notice when you stop catastrophizing over minor inconveniences.

4. Lifestyle Factors: Your Brain is Basically a High-Maintenance Pet

You wouldn't expect a plant to thrive on junk food, 3 hours of sleep, and a constant barrage of stress, right? Well, your brain isn't much different.

Your Prefrontal Cortex (PFC) and Amygdala have very different opinions when it comes to maintaining balance and well-being, and their preferences shape the way your Divine Council operates. One of the most effective ways to strengthen your PFC while keeping the Amygdala in check is exercise. Your PFC loves movement, as physical activity increases blood flow, enhances cognitive function, and reduces stress hormones. Meanwhile, the Amygdala hates it, because when stress levels drop, it loses its grip on emotional overreactions and impulsive decision-making. Exercise becomes a direct act of empowerment for your higher thinking, allowing the PFC to remain the leader of the council, rather than letting the Amygdala hijack the system with unnecessary anxiety or fear-driven responses.

Another crucial factor in maintaining optimal brain function is sleep. Think of your brain as an expensive smartphone—you wouldn't let it drain to 1% and expect it to work efficiently, right? Sleep is your brain's recharge cycle, consolidating memories, regulating emotions, and ensuring that your PFC stays in charge rather than allowing exhaustion to hand over control to the Amygdala. When you consistently get quality sleep, your Divine Council operates smoothly, enabling clear thinking, emotional stability, and a well-functioning memory system. On the other hand, sleep deprivation weakens your PFC, making it harder to control impulses, manage stress, or engage in deep thought—essentially leaving the Amygdala to run wild in a state of unchecked reactivity.

Speaking of stress, chronic stress is the equivalent of letting a circus take over your mind, with your Amygdala as the ringleader and your PFC struggling to keep the show under control. Long-term stress doesn't just cause emotional exhaustion—it actually shrinks your PFC, reducing your ability to think clearly and make rational decisions. If life keeps feeling like an endless performance of chaos and overwhelm , it may be time to fire the stress-clown and replace it with relaxation acts like mindfulness, deep breathing, or engaging in activities that bring a sense of peace. Stress management isn't just about feeling good—it's a direct strategy to protect and strengthen your PFC so it can continue to lead with wisdom and foresight.

Finally, nutrition is the foundation of how your body and mind function. Every bite of food you consume is a fuel source for your brain, influencing how effectively it can process thoughts, regulate emotions, and sustain energy throughout the day. High-quality, nutrient-dense foods provide the raw materials needed to keep your Divine Council operating at peak performance, while processed, artificial, or nutrient-deficient factory foods can cause sluggishness, brain fog, and emotional instability. In essence, what you eat determines how well your mind can function, making food not just a source of physical energy but a direct influence on how well your PFC can lead, how stable your Amygdala remains, and how harmoniously your Divine Council operates.

Final Thought: Your Brain is a Divine Council, Not a Battlefield

Beloved seeker, consider your inner Divine Council as the sacred microcosm within—a reflection of Life Itself. Just as the universe operates through an intricate web of energy and consciousness, so too does your inner system function as a harmonious ensemble of divine intelligence. Each member of this inner council, each Primary Node, is a vital component of your existence, working in unison to shape your reality.

The Prefrontal Cortex, like the wise council leader, is the beacon of discernment, clarity, and higher reasoning, ensuring that each decision is aligned with wisdom and foresight. The Amygdala, ever the fierce guardian, keeps you alert and aware, offering its primal strength to navigate the terrain of life. The Anterior Cingulate Cortex, the compassionate mediator, ensures that emotion and logic do not battle, but rather dance together in sacred harmony. The Insula, our subtle sensor, tunes you into the sacred vibrations of bodily awareness, allowing you to feel deeply connected to the present moment.

And beyond these sacred governing forces, your Primary Nodes function as the very operating system of your being, each module designed to unlock different realms of experience.

In the grand cosmic play, Life itself is the infinite programmer, writing the code of existence through the dance of these inner modules. When they operate in perfect harmony, miracles occur—each thought, each feeling, each sensation becomes an expression of divine creativity. It is as though the very fabric of your being aligns with the cosmic order, transforming ordinary moments into luminous experiences of grace and synchronicity.

But what happens when you step beyond all definitions, beyond identity, beyond limitations? Remember, when you meditate or practice mindfulness, you enter a space of being nothing— In that moment, your system becomes a blank slate, and the universe has full access to upgrade your divine code. This is true systemic and neurological independence—a liberation from the programs of the past, the conditioned mind, and the material laws that have kept you entangled. You step onto the real gameboard of life, where you are not bound by old rules, but instead, create your own. Here, you realize that your true self is not separate from the cosmos, and therefore, you can become anything.

Reflect upon this: when your inner Divine Council functions in unity, you become a channel through which Life manifests its boundless wonder. The seamless integration of logic, emotion, intuition, and cosmic intelligence is akin to a masterfully coded symphony, echoing the eternal truth that every cell, every breath, is an expression of the Divine. In such moments, the boundary between your inner world and the outer world dissolves, revealing the oneness of existence. You realize that you are not a mere observer, but an active co-creator in the cosmic dance—a realization that can transform each instant into a sacred celebration of Life Itself.

Thus, nurture and calibrate your inner modules with mindfulness, compassion, and awareness. In doing so, you align yourself with the divine flow of the universe. And remember, dear one, that even when the system seems to falter, it is merely a call for gentle reawakening—a reminder to pause, breathe, and reestablish the sacred dialogue within.

For when your inner council plays in concert with the cosmic rhythm, miracles are not just possible—they become your lived reality. And Life, in all its splendor, unfolds before you as the divine mystery it truly is.

How do you see the characters of the divine council now? Have they changed at all? In look? In personality? If they were all together on a television show, how would you script the series finale? How are they all going to go on and help you navigate your life moving forward? What have you learned that can help make it all work out perfectly?

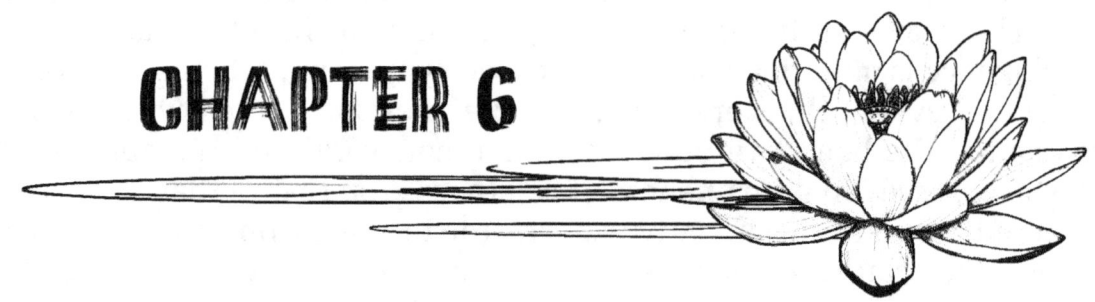

CHAPTER 6

The Inner Council: Accessing Life Itself Through Your Own Devine Assembly

There is no temple more sacred than the one within you. No priest, no book, and no ritual can replace the direct and personal communion with the Divine that occurs within the vast sanctum of your own consciousness. You are not separate from Life Itself, nor is Life Itself distant from you—rather, divinity is the very fabric of your being, encoded into every thought, every breath, and every sensation. Whether you call it Life Itself, Source, God, or the Infinite, you have been gifted with a divine council within that connects you to this ever-present reality.

Seeing Life Itself in Everything: Life as an Act of Worthy of Worship (Meditation)

The great sages, saints, and mystics of every tradition have echoed the same truth: Life Itself is everywhere, in everything, and can be known through direct experience.

The wind that brushes against your face is Life Itself moving through the world. The warmth of the sun on your skin is Life Itself's embrace. The challenges you face, the lessons you learn, the love you share—all of it is an unfolding of the divine. When you begin to see this, every interaction, every struggle, and every joy becomes sacred.

To worship is to recognize divinity in every moment, to allow yourself to be humbled by the grandeur of existence and to be uplifted by the realization that you are an essential part of it. Worship is gratitude for the breath that fills your lungs, for the mind that allows you to perceive beauty, and for the heart that enables you to feel love. Worship is learning to listen—to the silence between words, to the wisdom of your own soul, and to the quiet voice of the divine that has been speaking to you all along.

This is precisely why journaling with an emphasis on gratitude can be wildly transformative. When you start recognizing the divine in everything, the divine seems to want to show you even more. It's like when you invite your friends to your new apartment that you spent so much time organizing and making cozy: a true reflection of you. The friends who recognize and get excited about your space that you are creating, are the ones you can't wait to show the new remodel of the bathroom. Life Itself gets giddy when we pay attention to its grandeur and is delighted to show your Inner Council more of its infinite home.

"Where do I see Life Itself—and how does it speak to me?"

Take a moment to slow down and notice the sacred in the ordinary. Where do you feel the presence of something greater—in nature, in silence, in connection, in your breath? What moments of your life, however small or fleeting, have felt like a direct conversation with the divine? Let this entry be a meditation, a quiet worship, a gratitude offering to the grandeur already unfolding around and within you.

Unifying With the Higher Divine Assembly

As you cultivate this awareness, something miraculous happens: you begin to see yourself not just as an individual, but as a part of a much greater, more sophisticated divine assembly. Your personal inner council, once focused on everyday survival and decision-making, starts to attune itself to something far grander—a universal intelligence, a cosmic harmony that is always at work, orchestrating life in ways more intricate and beautiful than the human mind can fully comprehend.

You become aware that just as you have an inner council guiding you, so too does the universe operate under a divine order, a great intelligence that moves through all things. The same wisdom that governs the stars and the seasons is present within you. You are not merely a being navigating through life; you are Life itself, a unique expression of Life Itself's infinite consciousness.

When you surrender to this understanding, when you allow your own divine council to unify with this greater intelligence, your entire perception of yourself shifts. You no longer see yourself as small, limited, or separate. You recognize yourself as divine. You understand that you have never been alone, that guidance has always been within you, and that Life Itself has been whispering to you through your own thoughts, emotions, and intuitions.

This is the transformation that brings true encouragement. To see yourself as divine is to live with unwavering faith in your own purpose, to move through the world with grace, and to meet life's challenges with the confidence that you are eternally supported.

"What changes when I recognize myself as part of the divine assembly?"

Reflect on how your relationship with yourself and the universe shifts when you stop seeing yourself as separate and start seeing yourself as an expression of Life Itself. What does it feel like to know that the same intelligence that moves the stars also moves through you? How does this awareness change the way you listen, choose, and trust your path? Let this be a moment of reunion—with your inner council, with the higher divine order, and with the truth that you have always been held.

Embrace Your Divine Nature

You do not need permission to access Life Itself. You do not need intermediaries, rituals, or grand declarations. You need only to listen—to the divine council within you, to the sacred wisdom of your own heart, and to the unbroken presence of the Infinite in everything you see and experience.

Every moment is an opportunity to remember who you are. Every breath is an invitation to return to the divine. Every thought, every emotion, every experience is a thread in the sacred tapestry of your existence.

When you awaken to this truth, life ceases to be something happening to you—it becomes something happening through you. You become a living embodiment of Life Itself's presence, a vessel for divine wisdom, a mirror reflecting the infinite light of creation.

So walk forward with confidence. See the world as a sacred place. Honor your divine council, trust its wisdom, and recognize that you are already a part of something vast, luminous, and eternal.

You are not separate from Life Itself. You are Life Itself's expression. And when you realize this, truly realize it, Life Itself becomes a sacred masterpiece—an ongoing miracle of divine communion. You can honestly and humbly say goodbye to the ailments that have governed you for so long.

Breathe in: I am free from the patterns and definitions of the world.

Breathe Out: I am the one who creates my own reality.

"What would my life look like if I truly believed I am an expression of the Divine?"

Close your eyes. Breathe in: I am free from the patterns and definitions of the world. Breathe out: I am the one who creates my own reality. Now write—freely, honestly, and without restraint. How would your thoughts shift? What choices would you make? What fears would dissolve? Explore the version of yourself who walks as a conscious vessel of Life Itself, who no longer waits for permission to live fully, but simply remembers who they've always been.

CHAPTER 7

The Brave Art of Microscopically Honest Self-Creation: A Path to True Freedom

The beauty of life, in all its messiness, lies in one simple truth: Self-creation begins with self-honesty. But not just any honesty—the microscopic kind. It's about turning the lens inward, zeroing in on the smallest, often unnoticed details of your mind, heart, and actions. And trust me, this is where the magic happens.

We've all heard the phrase, "The truth will set you free," but let's get real—truth is not always a simple or comfortable thing to digest. In fact, most of us are running around with a handful of half-truths and well-meaning illusions we've created to make life easier, more palatable. But those half-truths are like little cracks in the foundation of your life. They're not harmless—they're subtle, they're sneaky, and they keep you from being fully yourself.

So, microscopic honesty is about looking at those cracks—those tiny, often uncomfortable details—and seeing them for what they are. You see, real freedom doesn't come from ignoring your imperfections. It comes from embracing them so deeply that they stop having power over you. The truth about who you really are—flaws and all—is the greatest gift you can give yourself. And here's the kicker: that's where your true strength lies.

"What truths about myself have I been avoiding—and what might shift if I face them with love?"

Take a breath and get curious. Not harsh. Not critical. Just honest. What small, quiet truths have been whispering beneath the surface—about your desires, your fears, your habits, or your needs? What would it feel like to look at them with compassion instead of judgment? Explore how embracing these "microscopic" truths might unlock a deeper freedom and allow a more authentic version of you to step forward.

Why Microscopically Honest Self-Creation Requires Bravery

Being honest with yourself isn't like posting a "motivational" quote on Instagram. It's not a grand declaration that you're going to "live your best life." It's not a moment of applause or recognition from the world. No, microscopic honesty is the quiet rebellion against the version of yourself that you've been hiding from. It's getting up close and personal with your fears, your faults, and those messy thoughts you're not sure you want to acknowledge.

Why is this so courageous? Because, in order to be microscopically honest, you have to strip away the layers of your carefully crafted self-image—the one that's been pieced together by family, society, and even your own ego. It's the true self that lies beneath all the masks that scares us.

We're terrified of seeing the truth about ourselves because it feels vulnerable, raw, and at times, ugly. But that's the ultimate courage: looking in the mirror without flinching, without turning away, and being willing to meet the truth head-on.

Think about it this way: When you're brutally honest with yourself about your patterns, behaviors, and beliefs, you no longer need to hide. And once you stop hiding, you get the unbelievable freedom to create the version of yourself that you truly desire—not the one dictated by the needs of others, not the one society expects, but the version that honors your true essence.

Here's a challenge, write down one thing that you have avoided being honest about yourself and deeply feel into how that avoidance grew into something more dramatic than you had anticipated. Remember the Petri dish?

The Role of Your Inner Divine Council in Practicing Microscopic Honesty

Your inner council—the Prefrontal Cortex (PFC), Amygdala, Anterior Cingulate Cortex (ACC), and Insula—help you navigate the process of being brutally honest with yourself.

- **The Amygdala:** Yes, the emotional firebrand of your system often wants to run and hide at the thought of uncovering truths that might be too painful or too difficult. But its job isn't to just react—it's to alert you to the danger. And the moment you face that danger head-on and let it pass through you, you are essentially neutralizing its power. The Amygdala, then, becomes an ally in the journey of truth, signaling where the emotional charge is, allowing you to address it instead of run from it.

- **The PFC:** This is your internal wise counselor, the one who can see things logically and with clarity. It's the part of you that can calmly say, "Alright, I see what's happening here. I'm going to walk through this truth, even if it makes me uncomfortable." Your PFC can help you manage the mental overload and keep your reactions in check when the truths are hard to swallow. It's the wise teacher that says, "Growth happens in discomfort. Let's take this one step at a time."

- **The ACC:** The balance-keeper between emotion and logic. It's the one that ensures you don't spiral into self-judgment when you see a truth about yourself that's difficult to accept. Instead, it helps you integrate the emotional response to truth with the logical understanding of your patterns. This balance allows you to process the discomfort without letting it overtake your mind or your heart. The ACC ensures that self-compassion is never too far from self-reflection.

- **The Insula:** Your body's internal sensor, detecting physical discomfort or resistance as you face the truth. If you feel tension in your chest or a lump in your throat as you confront an uncomfortable truth, the Insula is sending you a signal that something important is happening. Rather than running from it, you can lean into it, allowing yourself to fully feel the discomfort so you can move through it and ultimately release it.

Your inner council isn't here to make you comfortable all the time. Their job is to help you navigate the truth—no matter how it shows up. This team of divine counselors is the foundation of your bravery, helping you peel away the layers of illusion and face the most delicate parts of your being.

"How is my inner council guiding me toward deeper honesty?"

Invite each member of your divine inner council to speak. What is the Amygdala alerting you to—what emotional truth are you avoiding? What insight does the Prefrontal Cortex offer to help you walk through that discomfort with clarity? How does the ACC help you hold space for both emotion and logic without collapsing into judgment? What physical signals is the Insula sending you right now—what is your body trying to say?

Let each voice guide you into a deeper, more courageous layer of truth—and discover what shifts when all parts of you are heard, honored, and aligned.

The Practice of Microscopic Honesty

Now, let's talk about how you can cultivate this kind of microscopic honesty in your life. It's one thing to understand it; it's another thing to practice it consistently. Here's how to do it:

1. Commit to Self-Awareness: Start by regularly checking in with yourself. Ask the hard questions: "What am I really feeling right now? Why am I avoiding this particular issue? What's the underlying fear or belief that's driving this?" This requires stillness and reflection—creating time in your life to just sit with yourself and observe your thoughts and emotions.

How does it feel when you try to make this commitment of time for yourself? Do you feel empowered? Selfish? What can you do to truly commit to self-awaremess?

2. Don't Skip the Small Details: Truth doesn't always come in big, dramatic moments. Often, it's found in the quiet, overlooked corners of our lives. Pay attention to the small, seemingly insignificant moments where you hide or deny your truth. It might be the time you're unwilling to apologize, or the emotion you suppress when a friend says something you don't like. Microscopic honesty is found in the smallest of moments—when you allow yourself to feel what you truly feel and acknowledge what you truly think, without judgment.

Challenge yourself to truly be honest with yourself. Take the time to dive deep and actually write, say, or allow yourself to be fully aware of the things you've kept hidden in the deepest recesses of your mind. Trust yourself.

3. **Embrace the Discomfort:** When you feel uncomfortable with the truth, don't run from it. Sit with discomfort. This is where the Insula comes in—your body's feedback system. Tightness in your chest? A lump in your throat? It's your body's way of saying, "This truth is moving through you." Don't resist it. Let it be. And allow your mind and body to process it without turning to distractions.

"What am I afraid of?"

Allow yourself to truly feel your discomfort and note the sensations in your body and mind. Then, as you allow the truth to move through you, be aware of changes you feel as your mind and body process the new feelings.

4. **Reframe Your Narrative:** Often, we build stories around our discomforts. We tell ourselves that we're "too sensitive" or "not good enough." But what if those stories are just misunderstandings? When you get brutally honest with yourself, you realize that you have the power to rewrite your narrative. Microscopic honesty allows you to challenge the stories that no longer serve you and begin creating a new, more empowering one.

When you feel yourself falling back to the comfortable story you've always told yourself to explain why you've never faced the truths you're finding, what do you notice? How real is the story? Is it a misunderstanding? An excuse? How can you move past it and face the real truth?

5. Integrate Self-Compassion: Honesty without compassion can be harsh and unhelpful. But when you pair the brutal truth with kindness, you create a healthy environment for growth. The ACC ensures that you don't beat yourself up for the truths you uncover, but rather, you honor them as part of your human journey. You're learning and growing—not condemning yourself.

Can you feel your ACC go to work within your divine council? Are you allowing yourself the necessary level of grace for these truths you're forcing yourself to confront? If so, how does it feel? If not, how can you refocus your thoughts in a more healthy way?

The Freedom in Microscopic Honesty

The freedom of microscopic honesty lies in the authenticity it brings to your life. The more you see yourself, the more you can create a life that is true to your soul. When you begin to live with microscopic honesty, you unblock your path to deeper growth, fulfillment, and peace. You stop living in reaction to life and start creating it consciously, one honest moment at a time.

So, here's the challenge: Get microscopic. Turn your attention to the smallest details of your truth. And in doing so, you'll find that your life becomes a masterpiece—a life lived with bravery, authenticity, and soulful self-creation. You'll find that there really isn't a problem with how you've existed. You are not your own fault. Nothing is permanent.

Now, isn't that the kind of life worth living?

"What truths am I ready to see more clearly—no matter how small?"

Choose one area of your life—relationships, work, health, self-talk, or habits—and zoom in. What subtle patterns or quiet truths have you been glossing over? What happens when you look closer, with compassion instead of judgment? Write about what it would feel like to live each day as an act of microscopic honesty—where nothing is hidden, and everything becomes an opportunity for freedom, authenticity, and soulful self-creation.

Chapter 8

Cultivating Bravery:
The Art and Skill of Facing Life and Death

Bravery is often painted in broad strokes—our minds race to images of fearless warriors charging into battle, superheroes leaping into action, or a daring escape from certain doom. But real bravery, the kind that transforms your life and your spirit, is about the quiet, persistent ability to face uncertainty, change, and even fear, with a steady heart. It's about choosing courage even in the absence of certainty, knowing that the act of stepping forward, in itself, is the brave act.

With the knowledge we've gained about the inner workings of our Divine Council—your Prefrontal Cortex (PFC), Amygdala, Anterior Cingulate Cortex (ACC), and Insula—we can now see bravery not as a fleeting moment of exceptional courage, but as a skill that you can cultivate over time. Like any skill, it requires practice, refinement, and a certain level of self-awareness.

So, how do we develop the skill of bravery? It's about leaning into what we already know about our inner world and using it as a foundation. Let's dive in.

"What does bravery look like in the quiet moments of my life?"

Reflect on the kind of courage that doesn't make headlines—the courage to change, to tell the truth, to begin again, to feel fully, or to sit with discomfort. How have your inner council members—the PFC, Amygdala, ACC, and Insula—guided you through those brave, unseen moments? What does it mean to you to cultivate bravery not as a performance, but as a practice? Explore where in your life you're being invited to take one more steady step forward, even without certainty.

Step 1: Understand Your Inner Council and Recognize the Source of Your Fear

Before you can develop bravery, you first need to understand where your fear comes from and how your inner council responds to it. I am repeating myself over and over again intentionally because it's super important. Reminder: Think of the PFC, Amygdala, ACC, and Insula as a team of experts, each with their own job to do when it comes to navigating life's challenges.

- The Amygdala is your emotional sentinel, the first responder to any potential danger. It sends signals of fear and anxiety, alerting you to threats. When it's overactive, it makes mountains out of molehills, turning everyday stressors into life-or-death situations.

- The Prefrontal Cortex (PFC), on the other hand, is the logical strategist. It's the one who says, "Hold on, let's think this through before making a decision." When you feel fear, the PFC helps you decide whether you should truly run away or stay and face the challenge.

- The Anterior Cingulate Cortex (ACC) acts as the mediator or perfect parents, weighing both emotional reactions and rational thinking, ensuring balance. It brings a sense of harmony, reminding you to pause, breathe, and regulate your response, instead of reacting impulsively.

- And then, there's the Insula, the sensor, tuning into your physical and emotional sensations. It's the one that lets you know when something feels off in your body—tightness in your chest, a lump in your throat, or the sense of dread creeping in.

In every moment of fear, your Divine Council is already responding. The Amygdala jumps to conclusions, the PFC seeks logical calm, the ACC tries to balance things out, and the Insula checks in with your body. Bravery comes when you recognize how this internal team works together and how you can use their insights to make a more grounded decision.

Bravery begins with awareness—awareness of your inner council's roles, and awareness of the fear that's bubbling up within you.

"How does my inner council respond to fear—and how can I meet that fear with bravery?"

Think of a recent moment when fear showed up. What did your Amygdala react to? How did your PFC try to bring logic into the picture? What was your ACC doing to keep you balanced? What signals did your Insula send through your body? Now, imagine revisiting that moment with full awareness of your Divine Council. What would bravery look like—not as fearlessness, but as a conscious, grounded response guided by your inner wisdom?

Step 2: Embrace Fear as a Companion, Not the Enemy

Fear is a natural response to life's challenges, but it doesn't need to be something that stops you in your tracks. In fact, fear can be your greatest ally. The Amygdala is doing its job by alerting you to danger, but just because it's sending out a signal doesn't mean that signal is accurate. Fear is an invitation to engage with truth.

Here's where bravery as a skill begins to unfold: Instead of avoiding fear, learn to embrace it as part of the human experience. The key is to notice fear without being consumed by it. Let's say you're about to speak in front of a crowd or confront a difficult conversation. The Amygdala will likely be flashing red flags, urging you to turn and flee. But the PFC can help you reframe the situation: "I am in control here. This fear is just an old pattern. I can handle this."

When you acknowledge your fear without judgment, and decide to face it anyway, you are practicing courage. You're training your mind to choose action over avoidance, growth over stagnation.

It's important to remember: fear will never completely disappear. But over time, you'll develop a muscle that allows you to move forward in spite of it. The more you exercise this bravery, the easier it becomes.

"What fear am I ready to embrace—and what truth is it trying to show me?"

Think of a fear that tends to hold you back—not necessarily the biggest one, but one that shows up often. Instead of pushing it away, explore what it might be protecting or pointing you toward. How is your Amygdala doing its job, and how can your PFC help reframe the narrative? What would it feel like to treat fear not as a roadblock, but as a companion on your path—one that signals growth, not danger? Write from the space between fear and action, and explore what it means to choose courage anyway.

Step 3: Cultivate a Habit of Mindfulness—Bravery Needs Focused Attention

To develop bravery, you must also develop the ability to tune in—to be aware of your thoughts, emotions, and physical sensations in any given moment. This is where mindfulness practices come into play. Mindfulness is the skill of directing your attention with intention, focusing not just on the external world, but on the inner workings of your mind.

The ACC plays a huge role in this process. As the divine parent between your emotional and rational centers, the ACC helps you stay grounded in the present moment, without spiraling into worry about what might happen. It's the one that tells you, "Pause. Take a breath. You're okay right here, right now."

When you practice mindfulness, you're training your brain to recognize when fear is taking over and when you can take a moment to refocus. This allows you to respond to life rather than react. You start to recognize that your thoughts and feelings are just temporary waves, not fixed states of being. Bravery comes when you stop letting those waves dictate your course. By maintaining mindfulness, you strengthen your ability to face fear, not as a threat, but as a part of your experience.

"How can mindfulness help me stay brave in the face of fear?"

Recall a recent moment when fear, stress, or anxiety tried to take over. What was your mind doing? What was your body saying? How might the ACC have supported you if you had paused, breathed, and simply noticed the moment without judgment? Reflect on how focused attention—on breath, sensation, or presence—could have shifted your response. What simple mindfulness practices can you commit to, not as escapes, but as tools for grounding your bravery in the now?

Step 4: Strengthen Your Inner Council Through Reflection and Practice

The skill of bravery grows through consistent practice and self-reflection. After each courageous act, take a moment to reflect and give yourself an opportunity to tell yourself how proud you are of you!. Did you listen to the guidance of your inner council? Was there a moment when you let the Amygdala drive the decision instead of the PFC? Did the ACC step in and keep you calm when your body was reacting in panic? Bravo!

Over time, this reflection will allow you to fine-tune your inner team. You'll start to notice patterns in your responses and be able to adjust accordingly. It's the difference between being reactive and being proactive. Just like any skill, bravery improves with feedback. The more you face your fears and reflect on the outcomes, the more courageous you will become.

Here's an example: If you're afraid of confrontation, the first few times you engage in tough conversations, your Amygdala may make you want to bolt. But with each encounter, your PFC gets stronger, guiding you to stay calm and logical. The ACC gets better at sensing when the emotional charge is high and reminds you to take a step back. And the Insula keeps your body relaxed as you speak.

After a few attempts, you'll notice that you're handling those confrontations with more ease. The Divine Council has started to function in a more harmonious way, and bravery has become second nature.

"How has my inner council supported me in moments of bravery—and how can I help them grow stronger?"

Reflect on a recent or memorable moment when you acted with courage. Break it down: What did your Amygdala do? How did your PFC help you stay centered? Did your ACC step in to help you balance emotion and logic? What physical cues did your Insula reveal? Celebrate the parts of yourself that showed up bravely. Then, write about how you might support each member of your inner council to grow even stronger moving forward. What kind of feedback or encouragement do they need from you?

Step 5: Let Go of the Need for Perfection—Bravery is Messy

The most important thing to remember is that bravery is messy. You will fail. You will stumble. You will fall short sometimes. And that's okay. Real bravery is about showing up, even when you're afraid to fail, and choosing to keep going even when you do.

The PFC is your reminder here: bravery doesn't require perfection. It's about showing up with honesty, vulnerability, and strength, even in your messiest moments. After all, if the PFC can help you make decisions with clarity, even when the situation is uncertain, you can learn to make your way through life with bravery, regardless of the bumps in the road.

So, remember this: the skill of bravery is developed over time. It's about practicing it every single day. Whether you're facing small fears—like speaking up in a meeting—or big ones—like standing up for your beliefs or confronting your own mortality—bravery is the art of moving forward despite fear. The more you practice, the more you'll realize that the courage to live fully is already inside you, waiting for you to awaken it.

In the end, bravery is about the willingness to walk through it with your inner council at your side. So step forward with confidence, knowing that your brain is built for this. And when you feel the fear creeping in? Just take a breath, tune into your inner council, and remember that you are brave enough to face whatever comes your way. After all, the world needs your bravery now more than ever.

"What would it look like to be brave without needing to be perfect?"

Think of a time when you were hard on yourself for not getting something "just right" while trying to be courageous. How might your PFC reframe that experience as growth rather than failure? What if your stumbles were signs of strength, not weakness? Write a letter to yourself from the voice of your inner council—offering encouragement, perspective, and permission to be both brave and imperfect. Let it be messy. Let it be honest. Let it be enough.

Living in Chaos: The "Normal" Routine

Let's look around. How many of us feel like we're running a constant marathon of chaos—mentally, emotionally, and spiritually? We wake up to the alarm blaring, hustle through the day with our minds jumping from one crisis to the next, and then wonder why we're so tired and stressed by the time bedtime rolls around. Our inner worlds are like computer hard drives with a thousand tabs open, and we're too scared to close any of them because, well, what if we miss something important? Spoiler alert: the most important thing you're missing is the peace that could give your life (and yes, your eventual exit) some much-needed clarity.

This inner turmoil is so commonplace we don't even realize it's happening. It's almost like we're in a constant state of trying to "fix" everything, never quite at ease, always in the middle of some drama, always a little bit on edge. We live in a world that tells us we must always be "doing" and "achieving" something—but the truth is, we can't get to peace if we're always acting like there's a fire to put out.

This perpetual chaos is exactly what the Default Mode Network (DMN) thrives on. The DMN is responsible for mind-wandering, self-referential thinking, and rumination. It's a part of our brain that can keep us trapped in endless loops of thought, replaying the past or worrying about the future. And guess what? It's the same part of the brain that will keep us distracted when we're trying to find peace. When the DMN is overactive, it's like having a dozen sticky notes flying around in your brain. They clutter the space, making it harder to focus, to relax, or to just be. Practicing mindfulness and grounding techniques can help quiet the DMN and bring your awareness back to the present, allowing you to finally close some of those mental tabs.

"What tabs are open in my mind—and which ones am I ready to close?"

Take inventory of the mental chaos: what loops, worries, or internal dialogues are taking up space right now? Which ones are truly urgent, and which are running on autopilot? How might your life feel if you gave yourself permission to pause, to breathe, and to let a few of those tabs go—just for now? Reflect on how your inner world might shift if you stopped chasing peace and started creating it by simply being present.

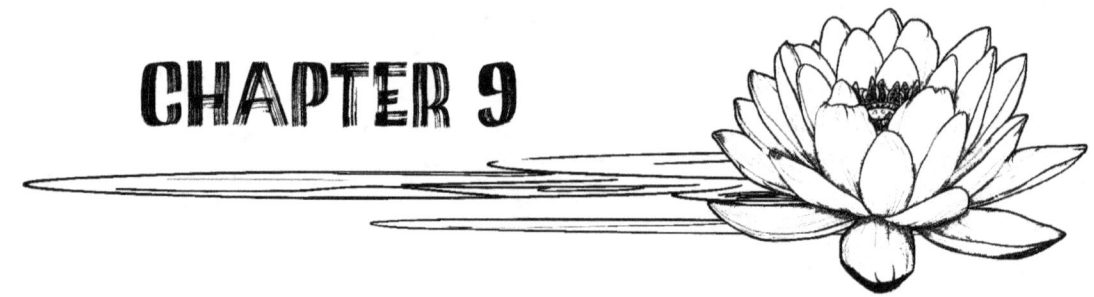

CHAPTER 9

Growing Up: The Inner Maturity Checklist

So, how do we begin to tackle this mess? It starts with growing up—yes, that means you, not just in years but in maturity. We need to start being emotionally, mentally, and spiritually responsible. It's time to deal with the inner clutter, the unresolved issues, and those little fears we've been stuffing in the back of our minds like they're old clothes we've outgrown but never bothered to donate. Growing up means facing your problems head-on instead of pretending they're not there. It means dealing with the inner noise so we can clear the path for peace.

The good news? You don't have to be perfect. You don't need to have everything figured out before you take a step toward peace. But you do need to commit to quieting the chaos within. It's like cleaning up your room before you invite people over: you don't have to go overboard, but it's a lot easier to have a good time when there's not a mountain of laundry on the couch.

Now, let's look at how this plays out in the brain: when we avoid growth, unresolved emotions and issues end up taking root in the body. These unresolved states often trigger the Amygdala—the part of your brain that handles emotional responses. The Amygdala is like your personal alarm system, but if it's constantly set off, it doesn't get to do its job properly. Instead of responding to actual threats, it starts reacting to every little thing with anxiety, stress, or even anger. Practicing self-regulation, through mindfulness, self-awareness, and therapy, can help you ease the burden on your Amygdala and give your entire system a chance to operate with more harmony. This is how we begin to grow into a state of peace—by tending to the areas of our lives that still need healing.

"What parts of me are still waiting to grow up—and how can I meet them with compassion?"

Take a moment to scan your inner world. Are there emotions you've been avoiding, fears you've tucked away, or habits that no longer reflect the person you're becoming? How might your Amygdala be overfiring not because you're broken, but because those inner rooms are still cluttered? What does it look like to "clean up" your emotional space—not perfectly, but intentionally? Write about one small step you're ready to take toward emotional maturity and inner peace.

Curating Harmony Within: The Inner Spa Treatment

Here's the thing: living peacefully (and eventually dying peacefully) is something you work at every single day. It's like giving your internal world a nice spa treatment—quieting your thoughts, letting go of grudges, and setting boundaries with that inner critic that insists you'll never get it right.

It starts with mindfulness—basically just paying attention to your thoughts without letting them drag you into a tornado of anxiety. It's the art of observing your mind without attaching to every drama or mini-crisis it throws at you. When you're able to practice mindfulness, you can start reprogramming the endless loops of negativity that run through your head. Think of it as an emotional cleanup job for your brain. Every time you notice yourself spiraling, you gently remind yourself, "Nope, we're not doing that today."

This inner "spa treatment" works wonders for our Prefrontal Cortex (PFC) and Anterior Cingulate Cortex (ACC). These brain regions are responsible for executive functions like decision-making, emotional regulation, and attention. When we practice mindfulness or self-regulation, we give these areas a chance to update their software, allowing us to make decisions from a place of calm and clarity instead of panic or emotional overload. Think of it like clearing away the digital clutter so the PFC can work more efficiently, helping you stay centered in the present moment.

Another part of this peaceful living gig is letting go of attachments. You know what I mean. That favorite pair of jeans you can't throw away because they were a gift (but you haven't worn them in five years). Those grudges you're secretly holding against people from ten years ago (even though they probably forgot you existed). The fear of losing control over every little thing. Letting go is about accepting that things, people, and situations are going to change—and that's okay. Life moves forward whether you hold on to it or not. The waves in the ocean will never cease.

"What inner clutter am I ready to release—and what would it feel like to live in harmony with myself?"

Imagine giving your inner world a full spa treatment. What thoughts, grudges, habits, or fears need to be gently scrubbed away? What's clogging up your PFC and ACC, making it harder for you to think clearly and respond with calm? Write about the emotional attachments you're ready to let go of—big or small—and envision what your inner life might feel like if it were lighter, softer, and more spacious. Let this be your invitation to curate peace from the inside out.

CHAPTER 10

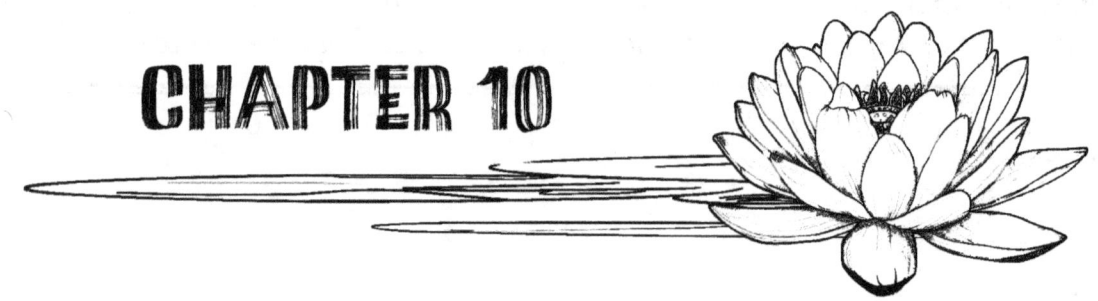

Rewiring Your Brain: The True Power of Meditation

Here's the thing: our brains are incredibly adaptable. Every time you sit down to meditate, you're retraining your brain to work better. Doing nothing and expecting nothing during meditation is how you allow Life Itself to do its work instead of you feeling like you need to hurry up and get better. Neuroplasticity is the fancy word for it, but remember, you have a divine council with the coolest tech to play with. Meditation is like installing a much-needed update that makes your team run smoother, faster, and with fewer errors.

Over time, mindfulness and meditation create new neural pathways that support emotional regulation, self-awareness, and clarity of thought. The more you practice, the more you build a brain that can respond to life rather than react to it. That's neurological independence in action—where you're not a slave to your impulses, stress, or anxiety. You're the boss of your mind, and it's working in perfect harmony with your body. So put down your body through meditation and pick it back up when it has been detailed and cleansed. This is literally how you clean up your act and grow up. Do nothing, trust Life Itself that the fruit that you produce is going to grow despite your need to "do" something.

"What might happen if I let go, sat still, and let Life Itself do the work?"

Reflect on your relationship with stillness. What comes up when you imagine meditating without trying to fix, improve, or strive? How would it feel to trust that your divine inner council—your PFC, Amygdala, ACC, and Insula—knows how to heal, balance, and rewire itself when you simply get out of the way? Write about the idea of meditation not as an effort, but as a surrender. What kind of life might grow from this kind of trust? What kind of brain might you build— gently, over time—by choosing stillness again and again?

The Power of a Calm, Focused Mind

When you practice meditation regularly, you're summoning the most powerful version of the divine council within your own mind. Imagine again: your Prefrontal Cortex (PFC), the wise strategist, sitting at the head of the table. Beside them, the Amygdala, once a fierce warrior reacting to every danger, is now a calm protector, using its power only when necessary. The Anterior Cingulate Cortex (ACC), your celestial mediator, is bridging the gap between rational decisions and emotional wisdom, ensuring that your actions are balanced and thoughtful. And the Insula, your sensitive inner sensor, is finely attuned to your body's needs, keeping you aware of your emotions without letting them overwhelm you. All these brain regions, once working independently or in chaos, are now co-ordinated—a finely tuned orchestra, working in harmony, united for one singular purpose: your well-being. When you meditate and let go, your inner council gets to meditate and let go.

When you meditate, you step into a position of authority, actively managing this dynamic team and lovingly giving them some well earned PTO. The more you practice, the more these councilors develop their synergy, and the more powerful and resilient you become. You're no longer at the mercy of your reactions. Instead, you're empowered to make conscious choices, choosing what deserves your attention, and letting go of what doesn't serve you. The noise and the chaos inside your mind begin to fade, replaced by a profound calmness, a steadiness that is unshaken by life's storms.

And don't mistake this calm for passivity. It's about being in full command of your emotional and mental landscape. Meditation doesn't promise to remove all the challenges and frustrations of life—because let's face it, life will throw curveballs, sometimes with perfect precision. But what meditation does is equip you with the tools to face them with unwavering clarity. Instead of being swept away by your emotions or overwhelmed by irrational thoughts, you develop an inner fortitude to stand tall, take a breath, and respond from a place of wisdom rather than impulse.

Imagine standing at the center of a storm. Winds howling, rain pouring, lightning striking all around you. Most people in this situation would be knocked off balance, reacting out of fear, panic, or frustration. But you, with a calm, focused mind, become like the eye of the storm—centered, clear, and undisturbed. You don't deny the storm's presence, but you know it's just a temporary disturbance. You have the clarity to see the bigger picture and the wisdom to navigate through it with purpose. You let go of trying to think you have any control of the storm in the first place. A storm is going to storm, a flower is going to flower, surrendering is making sure you don't keep pulling out your carrots to see if they're growing.

With regular practice, this becomes your default setting. The spaciousness that meditation cultivates allows you to live life with a level of awareness and perspective that most people can only dream of. No longer are you simply reacting to life; you're responding to it with full awareness, decisiveness, and deep understanding. You are unshaken by what's happening in the world. "Oh no! This politician is doing this, that corporation is doing that!" You no longer get pulled into the storm and realize the only place you have real influence anyway is within yourself.

When you develop a calm, focused mind, you are no longer controlled by your emotions or thoughts. You are their master, able to choose how you feel and how you think. This is the power of mindfulness and meditation—it's the key to breaking free from the cycle of reactive behavior and emotional turmoil.

This is the power of a calm, focused mind—it doesn't remove life's difficulties, but it makes you capable of meeting them head-on, with grace, strength, and most importantly, clarity. You are not at war with yourself anymore. You're in partnership with the most sophisticated, intelligent system known to humankind—your own brain. And in that partnership, miracles happen.

> *Life will still challenge you. But when you practice meditation, you'll meet those challenges not with hesitation, not with fear, but with clarity, confidence, and strength. You'll face every obstacle with the full force of your inner council behind you—the prefrontal cortex, your trusted decision-mak-*

er; the amygdala, now a loyal protector, not a panicked instigator; the ACC, your wise mediator; and the insula, your grounding body-sensor—all working together to help you navigate, adapt, and grow.

"What would my life feel like if I led it from the calm center of my mind?"

Visualize your inner Divine Council—PFC, Amygdala, ACC, and Insula—not in chaos, but in harmony. What changes in your daily life when your reactions slow down, your decisions come from clarity, and your body feels safe within your own awareness? Reflect on a time when you responded from stillness instead of panic. What did it teach you? How might your world transform if calm became your default setting—not because life got easier, but because you became more masterful in meeting it?

Why Wait? Start Your Inner Upgrade Today

Here's the beautiful truth: you don't need to wait for some mystical, magical moment of enlightenment to begin experiencing the incredible benefits of meditation. You can start right now. Yes, right at this very moment. You don't need to schedule an appointment with a guru, or climb a mountain (unless you really want to, of course). All you need to do is breathe. Take a deep breath. Close your eyes. Feel your body. And just like that, you've begun your inner upgrade. It's truly that simple. You are already on your way.

Even if you've never meditated before, don't let that intimidate you. This isn't about being perfect—it's about taking that first step. Start small, just a few minutes a day. And yes, your mind will wander. It's going to throw you a thousand thoughts, each one seemingly urgent, like a hyperactive puppy with too much energy. But don't stress. That's just your brain doing what it does best—thinking. The key is this: when your mind runs off in a million directions, you simply guide it back with patience. You lovingly steer it toward calmness, toward the breath. Like a child who is anxious to run into the swimming pool without its floaties, you gently bring the kiddo back and provide it with the tools to float and be safe. The kiddo is relaxed and can now enjoy the pool and so can the parent. Don't you think it would be unwise to yell, spank, or dropkick the kid into the pool to teach it a lesson? Gentleness—even toward your own thoughts—is the answer.

Over time, the inner council of your brain—the PFC, Amygdala, ACC, and Insula—will begin to fall into alignment. They'll start working together, not against each other. And with that cooperation comes a deeper peace and a more harmonious experience of life.

The Invitation

So, here's my heartfelt invitation to you: try it. Just a little mindfulness. Just a little meditation. You don't have to be perfect, and you definitely don't have to look like you've been meditating for years (unless you're into that "pretzel" position, in which case, more power to you!). What matters is that you do it regularly. Every time you meditate, you're nurturing peace in your inner world, teaching your brain how to function better, and creating more space for the things that truly matter. Like yourself.

Every breath, every moment of stillness, is a chance to tell your brain, "I'm in control." You're showing up for your inner council, letting your PFC make decisions, allowing your Amygdala to relax, and giving your ACC the chance to mediate between your thoughts and emotions. When you show up for them, they show up for you.

Now, imagine what your life would be like if your thoughts and emotions weren't constantly at war but instead were working in tandem for your highest good. What would it be like to meet stress with clarity instead of overwhelm? To approach challenges with focus instead of frustration? Write it down. It's all within your reach, right here and right now.

You've got this. All it takes is the courage to start. To take that first, gentle step. Mindfully. With a deep breath. And maybe, just maybe, with a little humor, because let's face it—life is far too short to take too seriously, especially when you have the power to take the reins of your own mind.

In the end, you're not just meditating to quiet your thoughts. You're cultivating the peaceful cooperation of your entire inner world—the calm wisdom of your PFC, the passionate insight of your Amygdala, the balanced mediation of your ACC, and the attuned sensing of your Insula. These are real, living forces within you, waiting for the moment when you say, "Let's work together." And once they do? The transformation is nothing short of miraculous.

So, what are you waiting for? Your inner council is ready to go. All you have to do is show up to your own frickin' meeting and you'll start to grow up! My apologies for the spicy language, I'm just so excited to meet you on the path.

"What happens when I finally show up for my own inner council?"

Picture it: *your PFC sitting calmly at the head of the table, your Amygdala taking a deep breath, your ACC harmonizing the room, and your Insula quietly tuning* *in. They've been waiting—patiently—for you to lead. What changes when you commit, not to perfection, but to presence? To just a few mindful minutes each day? Write about how your life might shift if you stop running from your mind and start working with it. What would it feel like to step into that meeting every day—not as a boss, but as a partner in peace?*

CHAPTER 11

Service to Others:
A Catalyst for
Neurological and Systemic Independence

Sometimes it can be extremely difficult to love yourself. Especially with the varieties of trauma that an individual can endure. We might not think that we ourselves are worthy of our own attention and affection.

When you choose to serve others, something magical happens—not just in the world around you, but within your own mind. It's easy to think of service as a selfless act aimed purely at benefiting others, but in truth, it's one of the most powerful ways to cultivate balance and independence within your own system. Service doesn't just strengthen your connections to others; it empowers your inner council—the wise, collaborative team of your Prefrontal Cortex (PFC), Amygdala, Anterior Cingulate Cortex (ACC), and Insula—to function with greater harmony, resilience, and clarity.

"How does serving others bring me closer to myself?"

Think of a moment when you extended kindness, support, or compassion to someone else—whether big or small. How did that act affect your inner world?

How did it shift the dynamic of your inner council—perhaps softening the Amygdala's defensiveness, activating the PFC's sense of purpose, calming the ACC's emotional balancing act, or attuning the Insula's sense of empathy? Reflect on how service can be both an outward offering and an inward healing. What would your life feel like if giving to others also meant gently returning home to yourself?

The Immediate Benefits of Service to Your Inner Council

When you serve others, you activate higher-level cognitive functions within your brain, those related to empathy, emotional regulation, and self-awareness. This isn't just charity—it's a neuroplastic workout for your mind.

PFC (Prefrontal Cortex): Service requires decision-making, planning, and organization. The PFC is the brain's executive manager, and when you engage in thoughtful, compassionate service, you're essentially giving it a workout. You're improving its ability to make wise decisions, prioritize tasks, and stay focused even in emotionally charged situations. In the process, you're strengthening your ability to respond, rather than react, to life's challenges.

Serving others often means stepping outside of your own personal bubble and recognizing that the world is larger than your own emotional responses. The Amygdala is the brain's alarm system, constantly scanning for threats and reacting with intensity. But when you put the needs of others before your own, the Amygdala learns to temper its responses. Instead of reacting impulsively, you begin to cultivate the capacity to respond with emotional intelligence. You train it to stay grounded, recognizing that true strength lies in resilience, not in reactivity.

The ACC acts as a mediator between your thoughts and emotions, bringing a sense of balance and stability to your mental processes. In the act of service, you strengthen the ACC by shifting your focus away from your own internal chatter and placing it on the needs of others. This shift reduces self-centered thinking and cultivates empathy, which, in turn, fosters mental clarity and inner peace. The ACC helps you hold both your emotions and your actions in check, allowing for a more fluid and balanced approach to life.

The Insula helps you tune into your body and emotions. When you serve others, particularly when you do so with compassion, the Insula strengthens its capacity to sense the emotional states of others, which in turn sharpens your self-awareness. By connecting with another person's experience, you gain deeper insight into your own emotional landscape, fostering emotional regulation and a balanced nervous system. Your sense of interconnection grows, leading to more harmony in your internal system.

"What does service awaken in me—and how does it transform my inner world?"

Reflect on a time when you helped someone or offered compassion, not out of obligation, but from a place of genuine care. What shifted in your PFC—did your sense of clarity or purpose increase? How did your Amygdala respond—did fear or stress soften? What did your ACC help you balance in that moment? And what signals did your Insula reveal about your own emotional body as you connected with someone else's experience? Explore how these inner transformations reveal that service is not just something you give—but something that gives back to your entire being.

The Ripple Effect: How Service Expands Your Systemic Independence

When you give, not only do you strengthen your inner council, but you also foster systemic independence—the ability to live in harmony with your own mind and the world around you. Here's how:

When you serve others, your ego—which can sometimes hijack your thoughts, emotions, and actions—takes a back seat. The act of selfless service creates space in your mind and heart to release the need for validation, control, or selfish desires. This freedom from ego allows your Prefrontal Cortex to step in with more clarity and logic, while your Amygdala is soothed, reducing impulsive emotional reactions. Your ACC stabilizes your inner world, helping you stay grounded, and your Insula fine-tunes your sensitivity to your own feelings and those of others.

Service often brings you face to face with hardship or discomfort, but this is where the magic happens. The brain's neuroplasticity means that by regularly choosing service, you train your brain to become more resilient. You learn how to handle emotional discomfort, challenge, and adversity with grace.

Your PFC helps you navigate difficult situations with wisdom and perspective, while your Amygdala remains less reactive, allowing you to stay focused on the bigger picture. The ACC and Insula help you stay emotionally balanced as you encounter the inevitable struggles of life. Every time you choose to serve, you add another layer of neuro-resilience, allowing you to live with greater inner peace and clarity.

Service builds a bridge between your inner world and the external world. When you serve others, you are essentially networking with Life Itself, connecting deeply with humanity and the broader universe. This sense of interconnectedness supports your brain's functioning, making it easier for the PFC, Amygdala, ACC, and Insula to work together with a shared sense of purpose and clarity.

As you cultivate empathy and compassion, your ACC thrives, creating greater internal harmony and enabling your mind and emotions to collaborate rather than conflict. This harmony extends outward, as you feel more connected to the people around you, the world, and ultimately, to Life Itself.

"How does service free me from ego and reconnect me with Life Itself?"

Think of a moment when serving someone else helped you drop your defenses—when you stopped thinking about how you were being seen, and started simply being present. How did that shift affect your inner council? Did your PFC guide you with more clarity? Did your Amygdala relax its grip? What balance did your ACC bring, and how did your Insula help you tune in, not just to others, but to your own emotional truth?

Explore how service softens ego, strengthens connection, and creates a state where your brain and spirit align in quiet, purposeful harmony with the world around you.

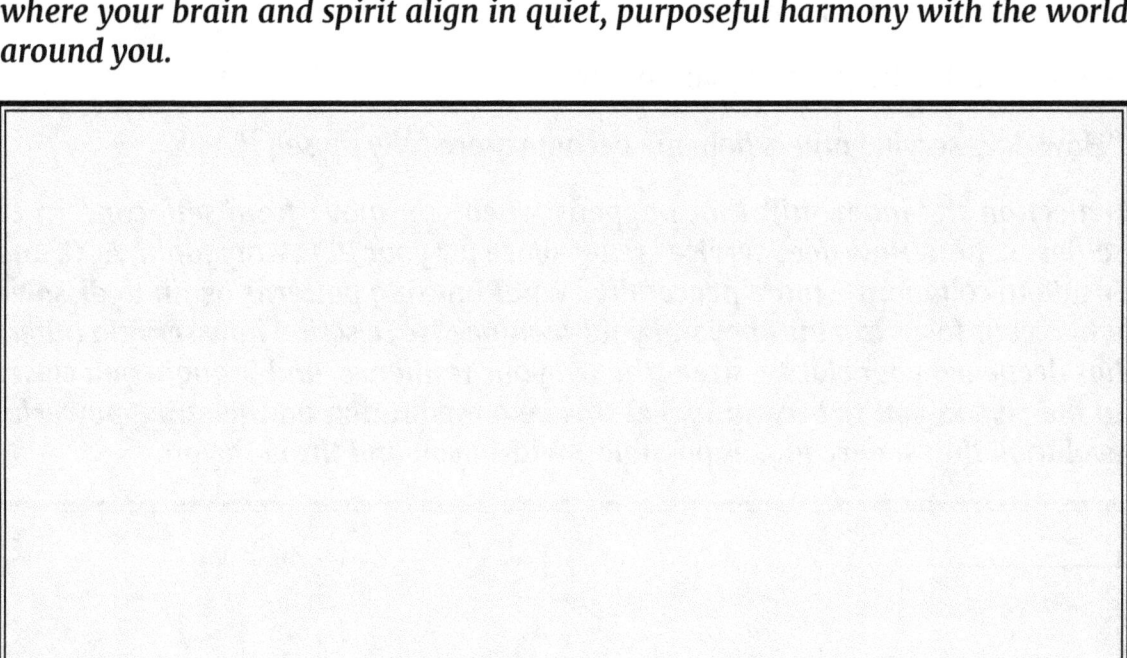

The Profound Synergy of Serving and Evolving

At the deepest level, service supports your journey toward neurological and systemic independence because it teaches you how to transcend the limiting patterns of self-centeredness and embrace a more holistic, interconnected worldview. When your inner council is working together in harmony—when your PFC, Amygdala, ACC, and Insula are in sync—you are in sync. You move through life with a sense of clarity, peace, and strength that is not easily shaken by external circumstances.

So, yes, service to others benefits more than just the people you help. It's a gift to yourself. It's an invitation for your inner council to unite in the most powerful way, harmonizing the forces within your mind and body that govern your perception of reality. It allows you to live with greater freedom, compassion, and clarity, creating a ripple effect of peace in your life, and in the world around you.

Serve, and in the process, you evolve.

"How does serving others help me become more fully myself?"

Reflect on the inner shift that happens when you move from self-concern to selfless action. How does service create space for your PFC, Amygdala, ACC, and Insula to collaborate more peacefully? What limiting patterns begin to dissolve when your focus expands beyond your own needs? Describe how serving others has deepened your clarity, strengthened your resilience, and brought you closer to the person you're becoming. Let this be a meditation on the quiet, powerful evolution that service makes possible—within you and through you.

CHAPTER 12

The True Meaning of Doing Your Best: A Vision for Systemic and Neurological Independence

In the grand dance of existence, every single one of us plays a vital role. We are not merely players in this cosmic drama; we are the creators, the alchemists of our own lives. The true meaning of "doing your best" is not about relentless striving to meet some arbitrary ideal. It's about returning to the perfect harmony that already exists within you. It's about choosing, moment by moment, to align with the most profound truth of all: you are already perfect—right here, right now.

If all you did in your life was to repeat the phrase: "I am perfect in this moment," You would eventually transform your thoughts into the most loving and compassionate friends. If you are reading this, in this precise moment, you are in complete alignment with the intentions of Life Itself. You are a good person in this moment, even if you have committed perceived atrocities in your past.

The pursuit of systemic and neurological independence is not about perfection in the conventional sense—it's not about becoming flawless or "fixed." It's about recognizing that your inner council, the divine assembly of your Prefrontal Cortex, Amygdala, Anterior Cingulate Cortex, and Insula, is inherently wise.

When you allow these forces to collaborate rather than compete, you will discover that you have always been whole, always been capable, and always been exactly who you needed to be. You're simply gaining skills in navigating your own system.

"What does it mean to me to be perfect in this moment?"

Let go of the usual definitions of success, healing, or "doing enough." Reflect on what shifts inside you when you repeat the phrase: "I am perfect in this moment." How does this truth feel in your PFC—your inner strategist? What happens to your Amygdala when it no longer needs to defend you? How does your ACC help you integrate this sense of inner peace, and what does your Insula reveal about the body's response to radical self-acceptance?

Write from the version of yourself who already is whole, and explore what life looks like when your goal is no longer to fix yourself, but to cooperate with the brilliance that's been within you all along.

Doing Your Best, The Heart of Love and Compassion

At its core, doing your best is about embodying love and compassion—not just for the world, but for yourself. It's about understanding that your mind, body, and spirit are interconnected in a beautiful system of balance. The work you do on the inside ripples outward, transforming not only how you relate to yourself but how you interact with the world around you. When you do your best, you are offering the world the highest version of yourself—a version that is not bound by fear, limitation, or old wounds.

What does it mean to do your best in this context? It means being gently, microscopically honest with yourself, allowing your inner wisdom to rise above the distractions and noise of daily life. It means embracing the imperfections, the doubts, and the chaos, not with judgment, but with compassionate curiosity.

Every time you choose to tune in to the deep, intelligent quiet within, you're strengthening the harmony of your inner council. And in doing so, you're becoming more of who you already are—a being of boundless potential, capable of profound peace and clarity. Gosh, you're cool. Do you feel it?

"What does it feel like when I'm truly doing my best—with love and compassion?"

Let go of the hustle, the perfectionism, the proving. Write from the place inside you that knows your best doesn't mean being flawless—it means being real, present, and open-hearted. What happens in your inner council when you show up with gentle honesty, when you let love guide your actions, and when you extend the same compassion inward that you offer to others?

Let this be a love letter to the version of you who's already doing enough. Already growing. Already whole. Gosh, you really are cool. Write it like you mean it.

Your Inner Council: A Path to Alignment

The beauty of systemic and neurological independence is that it empowers you to live from a place of alignment. When your mind is in alignment with your heart, when your emotions are in harmony with your thoughts, and when your body responds to your highest good, you unlock the magic of flow. You become the orchestrator of your own life, effortlessly navigating the complex systems of the mind and body.

The wisdom of your Prefrontal Cortex, with its ability to plan and make decisions with clarity, works in tandem with the fiery energy of the Amygdala, learning to respond with courage rather than react impulsively. The Anterior Cingulate Cortex (ACC), as your stabilizer, ensures that emotional chaos doesn't derail you, while the Insula keeps you attuned to your feelings and sensations, fostering self-awareness.

These parts of your brain are not isolated entities. They are your inner council, a divine collective working tirelessly to ensure that your every thought, feeling, and action is aligned with your highest potential. And in the moment you decide to listen to them, to give them room to collaborate in peace, you unlock neurological freedom—a freedom to live authentically, without the shackles of anxiety, fear, or reactive patterns.

"What does alignment feel like in my body, mind, and heart?"

Visualize your inner council—the wise PFC, the passionate Amygdala, the balancing ACC, and the attuned Insula—not as parts, but as a unified team. When they're in harmony, when they're working together instead of pulling you in different directions, what happens in your life? What does it feel like to live in alignment—with your thoughts, your emotions, and your deepest values all moving in sync? Describe this state. Let it be a blueprint for the life you're creating—one rooted in peace, flow, and conscious power.

The Freedom of Knowing You Are Already Whole

As a global citizen, it's easy to become entangled in the endless pursuit of external success, validation, or approval. But here's the radical truth: you are already whole. Your inner world, your divine council, is complete. The key to freedom, to peace, to neurological and systemic independence, lies not in changing who you are, but in remembering who you've always been.

You are already perfect. You do not need to add anything to your essence to be worthy of love or success. True love and compassion come from acknowledging this truth—by embracing yourself, fully and unapologetically, as you are. When you stop seeking external validation and turn inward, you open the gateway to a life of harmony, fulfillment, and inner peace.

This is what it means to do your best: to trust that your innate wisdom is enough, to know that your inner council has everything it needs to create the life you desire. Doing your best is not about competing with others or about becoming something you are not—it's about allowing yourself to be the most authentic, loving version of yourself that you already are.

"What if I stopped trying to become something—and simply remembered who I already am?"

Take a moment to sit with the truth that you are already whole. What thoughts or sensations arise in your body when you hear that? What shifts when you believe—even just for a breath—that you don't need to fix, prove, or add anything to be worthy? Let your inner council—your PFC, Amygdala, ACC, and Insula—speak from that place of wholeness. What do they say when you stop striving and start listening? Write as if you're writing from the center of your own completeness.

The Global Impact of Inner Peace

When you cultivate this kind of inner alignment, the effects are far-reaching. A peaceful mind creates peaceful actions. When you act from a place of love, compassion, and clarity, you influence the world in a ripple effect. You are the change. Your personal harmony becomes part of the collective, infusing your community, your family, your society, and eventually the globe, with the energy of peace.

It's a powerful, beautiful thing when we all begin to realize that the most important work we do is within. Our inner councils, united in wisdom, love, and balance, hold the key to a world where systemic independence isn't just an individual pursuit but a collective revolution. The peace you cultivate in yourself, in your daily practices of mindfulness, service, and self-love, becomes the foundation for a new way of living—for a world that thrives on collaboration, compassion, and understanding.

"How does my inner peace ripple out into the world?"

Imagine your inner council—aligned, grounded, and united. From this place of inner peace, how do you show up differently for others? How does your presence shift the energy of your home, your conversations, your community? Write about the ripple effect of your own harmony. How might your calm inspire calm in others? How does your compassion change the way conflict is met? Explore what it means to be a quiet revolution of peace—within and without.

A Call to Action: Do Your Best, Not Tomorrow, But Today

So, my fellow global citizen, the invitation is simple: start today. Begin by acknowledging that you are already perfect, right now, in this very moment. Trust in the wisdom of your inner council—the divine assembly within your brain. Lean into the practice of mindfulness, self-reflection, and service. Allow the PFC, Amygdala, ACC, and Insula to guide you toward greater clarity and balance. You are already whole, already wise, already everything you need to be.

There is no need for external validation or comparison. The world is waiting for you to show up as the perfect, divine version of yourself—ready to bring peace, wisdom, and love into the world, one small action at a time.

You are perfect, you are complete, and you have everything you need to create the life you desire. The journey of systemic and neurological independence is not a distant goal—it is your birthright. And all it takes to claim it is to begin today, right now, in this moment of inner harmony.

Do your best—not because you need to prove anything, but because the world is waiting for your unique light to shine.

"What does it look like to do my best—today?"

Not tomorrow. Not when everything is perfect. Today. In this moment. What small, intentional act can you take to align with your inner council and express the peace, wisdom, and love that already live inside you? What does your PFC suggest as your next clear step? What reassurance does your Amygdala need to relax? How does your ACC help you hold grace and emotion at once? And what is your Insula whispering about what your body truly needs today?

Write it all down. This is the beginning of living as the whole, perfect version of yourself—not someday, but now.

CHAPTER 13

The Power of Systemic and Neurological Independence in Intimate and Familial Relationships:
A Guide to Inner Harmony and Connection

Alright, let's get real for a moment. Intimate relationships—whether with a partner, family, or even friends—can sometimes feel like you're juggling flaming swords while riding a unicycle. There's passion, there's friction, and more than once you might find yourself wondering why on earth you're voluntarily signing up for this circus. But here's the kicker: it doesn't have to be so chaotic. In fact, when you start to cultivate systemic and neurological independence, you might just find that the whole act gets a whole lot smoother.

Let's talk about what that means, with a little help from our trusty inner council.

"How does my inner council help me love—and be loved—with more clarity and peace?"

Think about a close relationship in your life that sometimes challenges you. How might your Prefrontal Cortex (PFC) offer clarity when things feel heated? What role does your Amygdala play when old wounds are triggered, and how could it be gently soothed? How does your ACC step in to help you hold both emotion and logic in the same space? And how might your Insula deepen your empathy by helping you sense your own and others' emotional states more clearly?

Write about how systemic and neurological independence can shift the dynamics in your relationships—from reactive to responsive, from chaotic to connected. What might harmony in love really look like when your inner council is leading the way?

Embracing Relationships as a Divine Council of Exploration

I'm lovingly reminding you once again: your Prefrontal Cortex (PFC), Amygdala, Anterior Cingulate Cortex (ACC), and Insula all share one sacred truth—they are devoted to you. There is literally nobody else that they can worship or pay attention to. Even when their voices seem at odds, even when one shouts while another whispers, their purpose is singular: to guide you, to protect you, and to help you navigate this world with wisdom and heart.

And just like your own Divine Council, every person you meet brings their own unique constellation of inner allies. Every relationship—whether intimate, familial, or fleeting—is an invitation to see beyond your own lens, to step into the symphony of another's inner world. The more in tune you are with your neurological independence, the more gracefully you move through life's inevitable storms—not just for yourself, but for the people who journey alongside you.

"What if every relationship is a meeting of divine councils?"

Reflect on someone close to you—a partner, a family member, a friend—and imagine their inner council sitting across from yours. How might their Amygdala be reacting in moments of tension? What is their PFC trying to say beneath the surface? Can you sense the balancing effort of their ACC, or the emotional waves picked up by their Insula?

Now, come back to your own divine assembly. How can your council help you meet theirs with more compassion, curiosity, and understanding? Write about what it means to engage in relationship as a sacred exchange—where inner worlds collaborate instead of clash.

From Inner Harmony to Outer Connection

Mindfulness and meditation are not just personal practices; they are sacred acts of attunement. They give your inner council the space to collaborate rather than compete, to respond rather than react. When your council moves as one—balancing logic, emotion, intuition, and awareness—something profound happens:

Your reactions soften. The knee-jerk defenses, the old stories, the emotional floods—they lose their grip.

Your perspective widens. You begin to see others, not just through the filter of your own experience, but with true presence.

Compassion deepens. You recognize that every person carries their own council, their own struggles, their own victories.

In loving relationships built on systemic and neurological independence, something beautiful unfolds: you gain access to another perfect team of council members. Your partner, your friends, your family—they are not just companions; they are portals to new dimensions of perception. Every interaction is an opportunity to experience reality through a different facet of Life Itself. That's the whole goal of Life Itself, to explore how to live in infinite ways, there's truly no place to impose morality or judgment in this perspective. Infinite diversity, infinite amounts of lifestyles.

"What shifts in my relationships when I see others as divine councils too?"

Think about someone close to you whose behavior sometimes confuses or frustrates you. Now imagine their inner council—their PFC trying to think clearly, their Amygdala flaring up, their ACC struggling to find balance, their Insula overwhelmed with sensation. What changes when you stop expecting perfection and start seeing the sacred process at work in them, just as it is in you?

Write about how this perspective widens your understanding, softens your heart, and turns every relationship into a shared journey of mutual attunement and discovery. How might honoring both councils—yours and theirs—create a new kind of connection?

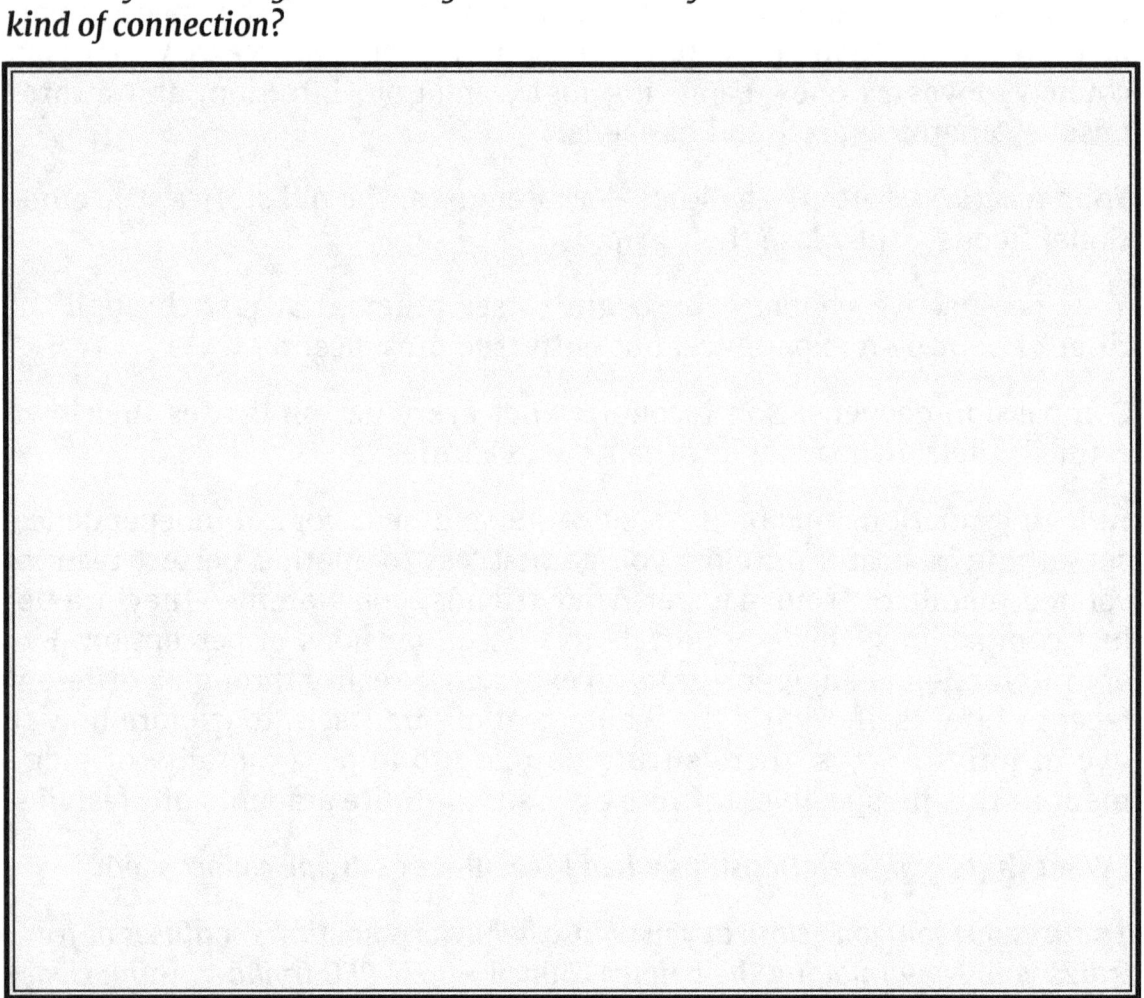

Same Team. We Always Have Been.

When you see each relationship as an extension of the grand cosmic dance, you begin to love people as they are—in their skin suits, with all their quirks, contradictions, and divine complexity. The illusion of separateness fades, and what remains is curiosity, collaboration, and a deeper reverence for the perspectives that are not your own.

We are not meant to do this alone. We were never meant to walk through life only seeing through our own eyes. When we embrace relationships as an expansion of consciousness itself, we grow not just in love, but in depth, in understanding, in evolution.

So let's do this together. Let's grow up with our most beloved—not just in age, but in awareness. Let's welcome every mind we meet as a sacred invitation to experience more of this universe than we ever could alone.

Because we are, and have always been, on the same team.

"What does it mean to truly be on the same team?"

Think of someone with whom you've shared both challenge and love. What happens when you see them not as opposition, not even as separate—but as a co-creator on the journey of consciousness? Imagine your inner council sitting beside theirs, not debating, but collaborating. What could shift if you treated every interaction as a sacred chance to grow together? Write about how this perspective changes the way you love, listen, and live. How does it feel to remember that we were never meant to do this alone?

Why Systemic Independence Improves Relationships

Think about it this way: relationships are like a dance. And while we all love a good waltz, it's hard to get your partner in sync if you're constantly tripping over your own feet. That's where systemic independence comes into play. By strengthening your ability to regulate your mind and emotions, you become a better dance partner in life.

Your PFC, the decision-maker, is able to make thoughtful choices—like choosing not to escalate an argument because you recognize it's not the time or place. Your Amygdala, the emotional powerhouse, learns to not react to every little irritant with the intensity of a volcano eruption. Instead, it listens to your ACC, which steps in like a wise mediator to ensure that emotions don't overwhelm logic. The Insula, your inner empath, helps you stay attuned to the feelings of those around you, allowing you to be more sensitive and considerate in your interactions.

With this kind of neurological independence, you stop fighting yourself and start working together—your brain and your relationships, that is. The more aligned your inner world is, the more peaceful your outer world becomes, especially when it comes to the people who matter most.

"How does my inner alignment shape the way I show up in my relationships?"

Picture a recent moment of tension or misunderstanding with someone close to you. Now revisit it with your inner council fully engaged—your PFC offering calm perspective, your Amygdala softened and less reactive, your ACC helping you hold both emotion and logic, and your Insula tuning you into what both of you were feeling.

Write about how the outcome might have changed if your system was working in harmony. How could systemic independence—grounded in awareness, regulation, and compassion—support deeper connection, even in the hard moments?

Loneliness in the Physical World? You've Got This

Now, let's be real again: loneliness is tough. It can feel like you're stuck in a room full of people but still isolated in your own little bubble. In an age of constant connectivity, being physically alone—whether you're living solo or just having a moment of solitude—can feel like a modern paradox. But here's the secret: when you cultivate systemic and neurological independence, you realize that loneliness is not your true state.

Your inner council is always there, waiting to guide you. The more you practice mindfulness, the more you realize that you're never truly alone. Your PFC is constantly working to help you see the bigger picture of your life, your Amygdala is learning to take a back seat, and your ACC is harmonizing your emotions, allowing you to embrace peace and connection within yourself. And don't forget the Insula, who keeps you connected to your own body and emotions, reminding you that you are always, always present in the here and now.

In this inner peace, you start to recognize that you are whole and complete as you are. And once you feel this deeply, you realize that your need for external validation—is not what ultimately sustains you. You become more at peace with your own company.

And guess what? When you're at peace with yourself, you become more attractive, more magnetic to others. It's like walking into a room with a calm energy that invites others to approach. Relationships thrive when we are not clinging to them for validation but instead offering love, connection, and support from a place of completeness.

"What does it feel like to truly enjoy my own company?"

Explore a moment—real or imagined—where you're completely at peace with being alone. No phone, no distractions, just you and your inner council. What are they doing? What are they saying? How does your PFC guide your thoughts gently? How does your Amygdala settle, knowing there's no threat in solitude? How does your ACC keep your emotions in balance, and how does your Insula help you feel rooted and alive in your own body?

Write about how solitude can shift from emptiness to intimacy—from loneliness to self-communion. What gifts become available when you realize you've never truly been alone?

Preparing for Right Relationship

Coming to resonate at the level you hope to be in partnership. Having patience to become instead of looking for others make us into something else. Relationships are classes not energy sources. Loving isn't owning or possessing but wondering (worshipping) the creative force in another form (any form).

"*How can I prepare myself to resonate with the kind of love I hope to receive?*"

Reflect on the kind of relationship you long for—not in terms of what someone else gives you, but in terms of how you show up. What inner qualities are you cultivating to match the energy of that love? How can your inner council help you become whole, patient, and grounded enough to meet love as a companion, not a crutch?

Write about the shift from seeking relationship to becoming ready for it. What changes when you stop looking for someone to complete you and instead prepare to meet love as a class, a wonder, a shared act of worship toward Life Itself in another form?

Building Deeper Connection in Relationships

Of course, practicing this inner work doesn't mean you'll never encounter bumps in the road. (Because, let's face it, relationships can be interesting.) However, when you understand that the foundation of every relationship starts within you, the challenges become less daunting. When your PFC and Amygdala are working together, you can face conflicts with clarity and compassion. When the ACC is on point, you can listen without judgment, and when the Insula is in tune, you can empathize deeply, without losing yourself in the emotional tides.

When you cultivate peace within, you attract peace without. You become the calm in the storm of relationships, the solid ground when others around you are feeling shaky. And the beauty is, this calm doesn't just benefit you—it benefits those around you. You become a support, a pillar, a source of grounded energy that others can lean on, without feeling overwhelmed by your own inner turmoil. You start to learn that other people's feelings, emotions, dysregulation, have nothing to do with you. How nice would it be if we didn't take each others' baggage so personally? Write it down.

"What changes when I stop taking other people's emotions personally?"

Think of a recent situation where someone close to you was upset, reactive, or overwhelmed. Now imagine meeting that moment with a calm, regulated inner council—your PFC offering grounded clarity, your Amygdala staying cool, your ACC mediating emotion and empathy, and your Insula helping you stay attuned without losing yourself.

Write about how this inner alignment shifts your experience in relationships. What does it feel like to hold space for someone else's storm without making it your own? How does this kind of presence deepen your connection, while preserving your peace?

You Are Never Truly Alone—And You've Got the Best Team in Your Brain

If you're feeling lonely, remember: you've got an entire divine council within you, always at your disposal. It's like having a group of loving, wise advisors ready to guide you through life's challenges. So, whether you're living alone or navigating complicated family dynamics, know that you have a powerful support system inside, ready to help you connect more deeply with yourself and others.

And if you ever find yourself struggling with feelings of isolation, just remember: you are always a breath away from reconnecting with your divine team. Whether it's through a moment of mindful breathing, a quick meditation, or simply taking a pause to listen to your body, your inner council is right there, waiting for you to tap into their wisdom.

"How can I deepen my connection with the divine team within me?"

When the world feels distant or your heart feels isolated, what does your inner council want you to remember? What reassurance does your PFC offer? How does your Amygdala calm when it knows it's not alone? How does your ACC help you feel balanced in moments of emotional disconnection, and how does your Insula draw you back into your body with gentleness?

Write about the sacred relationship you have with yourself. How might your life change if you truly believed that your most powerful support system lives within you—always present, always wise, always on your side?

A Final Word on Interpersonal Mastery

So, here's the takeaway: systemic and neurological independence is the secret sauce to healthier, more harmonious relationships—with yourself and others. By giving your inner council the space to collaborate, you naturally become a more balanced, compassionate, and understanding individual. You don't have to solve all the world's relationship problems in one go, but by doing the inner work, you become the change.

And if you're feeling lonely, just remember: peace starts within. Your brain has your back, and with a little practice, you'll find that your relationships—whether intimate or familial—become smoother, richer, and more fulfilling. So let's get that inner council to work! And by work, I mean give that inner council a vacation from your old script. We all operate much more efficiently after a day on the beach or a hike in the woods. Your relationships are waiting, and they're about to get a whole lot better.

"What would it look like to give my inner council a vacation from my old story?"

Think of the outdated beliefs or emotional scripts that have been running the show in your relationships—stories about your worth, your role, or how love "should" look. What if your PFC, Amygdala, ACC, and Insula didn't have to keep reacting to that old script? What would they do with a little more peace, space, and trust?

Write about what it might feel like to live—and love—from a fresh page, with your inner council relaxed, restored, and ready to co-create deeper, more joyful relationships. What would your connections look like if you led with inner harmony first?

CHAPTER 14

Systemic and Neurological Independence: The Ultimate Form of Peaceful Protest (No Cardboard Signs Needed)

The Unseen Cost of Aggression: Why Fighting Fire With Fire Only Burns Us All

In a world that is often on the edge of tension, it's easy to think that the only way to make a difference is through aggression, loud protests, or harsh confrontation. It feels powerful, doesn't it? To fight fire with fire. To scream in defiance. To lash out. But here's the truth that many forget: fighting fire with fire doesn't extinguish the flames—it makes them burn higher and hotter.

When we respond to aggression with aggression, whether it's on the individual, societal, or global level, we're doing nothing but feeding the fire. We're igniting a cycle of endless conflict, misunderstanding, fear and pain. It's a cycle that keeps us stuck, shackled by our own emotions, and blind to the potential of a better way—a way that can bring real, lasting change.

When we engage with the world from a place of aggression, our Amygdala dominates, and the PFC—the voice of reason—is drowned out. It's like a team of experts suddenly being overrun by a single loud, unruly voice that won't listen to the rest. Does that sound familiar? Can you observe how a single person (public or personal) can get the Amygdala of everyone around them to start going ballistic?

Write it down and possibly try to prove this concept wrong. Are there any scenarios where an amygdala dominant brain has created more peace and love for those around them?

The Vicious Cycle of Aggression

When one person gets angry and aggressive, others often mirror that response. The cycle intensifies. Someone yells, so someone else yells back. Voices escalate. Anger rises. The mind shuts down, and what could have been a thoughtful, compassionate exchange devolves into chaos.

When we engage in aggression, we get trapped in a loop that goes nowhere. The more we fight, the more we escalate. The Amygdala thrives in this environment—it feeds off emotional reactions, fear, and heightened intensity. But the PFC, the wise, composed brain leader, can't function well in such a charged atmosphere. The ACC, the mediator, is overwhelmed, unable to calm the situation. The Insula, which helps us process emotions and understand others' feelings, becomes so flooded with negative energy that it can no longer empathize. What was meant to be a solution becomes an out-of-control chain of events.

When we respond with aggression, we're contributing to the breakdown of human connection. We're abandoning the deeper possibility of peace, of understanding, of working together towards something bigger than ourselves. Aggression blinds us to the beauty of compassion. It clouds our judgment, leaving us focused only on defending our own perceived rightness and ignoring the reality that we are all in this together.

"What happens when I break the cycle of aggression instead of feeding it?"

Reflect on a moment when conflict escalated—when emotions flared and connection broke down. What was your Amygdala doing? Could your PFC get a word in? How might your ACC have helped mediate if given space? And what was your Insula trying to feel beneath the noise?

Now imagine pausing in that moment—choosing curiosity over control, compassion over reaction. Write about how breaking the cycle not only softens the situation but protects the deeper connection. What new kind of strength arises when you choose peace over power?

The Devolution of Humanity

Every time we resort to aggression, we degrade the very essence of what it means to be human. When we lose control of our emotions and let rage guide us, we step further away from the capacity for empathy, reason, and love. We deny ourselves the gifts of wisdom and deep connection.

Aggression doesn't evolve us. It devolves us. Think about it—when humans react with violence, they are simply mimicking the behavior of animals in the wild. But we are not animals. We are humans, with the potential for self-reflection, empathy, and understanding. We have the power to rise above knee-jerk reactions. We have the ability to create and build, not destroy.

When our brains are filled with emotional fire and chaos, we lose access to the higher faculties of reasoning, compassion, and problem-solving. The PFC gets short-circuited, the ACC can't mediate, and the Insula loses touch with the delicate nuances of emotional experience. As a result, we can't solve the real problems that need our attention. Instead of moving forward as a species, we're stuck fighting the same battles, repeating the same cycles of anger and misunderstanding.

"What does it mean to evolve beyond aggression?"

Think of a time when anger or conflict pulled you into a reactive state—when you felt yourself devolve into fight mode. What did it cost you? How did it affect your PFC, your ACC, your Insula, your ability to love or lead?

Now, envision a different path: one where emotional mastery, self-reflection, and empathy guide your response. What would it look like to become more human in those moments—not less? Write about what it means to choose evolution over reaction, and how you might contribute to humanity's healing by choosing to pause, reflect, and rise.

Peaceful Protest: The Most Revolutionary Act

Here's the golden truth: true power, true change, comes from within. The most profound revolution we can participate in is not one that is fought on the streets with signs, shouts, and violence. The real revolution is one of the heart. It's the choice to live from a place of peace, even in the midst of chaos. It's about peaceful protest—a protest that doesn't feed the fire of aggression but douses it with wisdom, mindfulness, and love.

You do not need to raise your voice in anger to be heard. When we choose peace, we step into our power. When we choose calm, we elevate our ability to reason and solve problems. We begin to dismantle the chaos and replace it with collaboration, with understanding. The most powerful form of protest is one that refuses to be sucked into the cycle of violence and anger. It is the protest of mental clarity, of emotional regulation, and of unwavering calm in the face of stormy winds. The wise eagle in the sky doesn't play in the mud with pigs. The unfortunate reason is that pigs enjoy that environment and will beat the eagle up with experience.

Instead of contributing to the noise, you become calm in the storm—the person who, through their actions, proves that it's possible to stay grounded amidst the chaos. When you resist the temptation to shout and lash out, you send a message far more powerful than any sign can convey. Your actions, your calm demeanor, your ability to pause and think before reacting, speak louder than any protest could ever hope to.

"What does peaceful protest look like in my everyday life?"

Think about a situation—personal or collective—where anger, conflict, or chaos is the default. How could your choice to remain grounded, mindful, and calm become a quiet act of revolution? How might your inner council—with your PFC offering clarity, your Amygdala tempered, your ACC balancing heart and mind, and your Insula tuned to the truth—lead you to respond in a way that heals rather than harms?

Write about what it means to embody peaceful protest—not through silence, but through intentional, loving presence. What power do you hold when you stop playing in the mud and start soaring like the eagle?

True Strength: Non-Violent Action is the Most Powerful Form of Change

Violence doesn't just harm others—it harms you, too. It harms your mind, your health, and your ability to think clearly. True strength lies in being able to remain calm and collected in the face of adversity. The real strength comes when you don't let the world dictate how you feel. You decide how you will react, and you choose peace over war, wisdom over impulsive aggression.

When you allow your inner council—your PFC, Amygdala, ACC, and Insula—to collaborate, you access the most powerful tool available to you: your own peaceful, focused mind. You stop being swept away by the flood of negative emotions. Instead, you respond with purpose, with clarity, and with love.

When you choose to live from this place of peace, you are not just changing yourself. You are affecting those around you. Your peaceful presence, your ability to maintain calm, sends a ripple effect into the world. People notice. They feel it. They might not understand why, but they feel the difference when you walk into a room with a centered, calm energy. You become the change you wish to see in the world—not through shouting, not through fighting, but through embodying the very peace you want others to experience.

"What does true strength look like when I choose peace over reaction?"

Think of a moment when you could have lashed out but didn't—or a moment when you wish you had paused instead of reacting. How might your inner council have helped you navigate that moment differently? What strength might your PFC have offered? What might your Amygdala have needed to feel safe? How could your ACC and Insula have helped you respond with compassion and presence?

Write about what it means to carry peaceful power—not passive, but potent. What kind of ripple could your calm create in your family, your relationships, your community? What does it mean to be a revolution of clarity and love in a reactive world?

The True Power of Non-Aggression: Transforming Society

Imagine a world where, instead of shouting at each other, we listened more deeply. Imagine a world where, instead of responding to anger with more anger, we chose to understand first, to pause and breathe before reacting. Imagine if we, as a collective, chose to respond to the chaos of the world with calmness, to transform the inner turbulence into a force for positive change. What would the world look like then?

It would look like freedom—freedom from the endless cycle of conflict. It would look like harmony, not just within individuals but between us all. True protest is not loud or violent. It's the quiet rebellion of the heart. It's the decision to refuse the emotional chaos and to remain calm, to remain grounded, to remain human.

So, the next time the world calls you to shout, to fight, to raise your voice in anger, remember this: the real revolution is happening inside you. Choose peace. Choose understanding. And watch how the world changes—one calm, focused mind at a time. If everyone chooses to ignore the tantrum, it loses fuel. If you don't like something in the world, I encourage you to completely unsubscribe.

"What kind of world am I helping create by choosing non-aggression?"

Imagine a society where calm minds outnumber reactive ones—where clarity, presence, and understanding guide our responses to conflict. What role does your inner council play in building that vision? How does your PFC lead with wisdom? How does your Amygdala surrender its need to escalate? How do your ACC and Insula anchor you in balance and empathy?

Write about the revolution inside you. What happens in your relationships, your community, your world, when you unsubscribe from chaos and commit to peace as a quiet, steady act of change?

CHAPTER 15

Honoring Life Itself Through Reframing Death

Now that we've received a basic understanding of the benefits of systemic and neurological dependence, let's finally have the conversation regarding grief and death.

The great spiritual adepts throughout history, from the ancient sages of the East to the mystics of the West, have universally spoken of death not as an end, but as a profound and transformative passage. To truly understand death is to unlock the deepest mysteries of Life Itself. It is in comprehending the nature of death that we gain clarity about the true nature of existence—about who we are, why we are here, and where we are going.

At first glance, death seems like a shadow that casts fear over our lives. It threatens to undo everything we cherish, to take away the people we love, and to put an inevitable end to the experience of being human. Yet, the great wisdom traditions remind us that death is not a void, but a doorway—an invitation into the infinite realms of existence that lie beyond the material world.

"What shifts in me when I see death as a doorway, not an ending?"

Reflect on your current relationship with the idea of death—whether it brings fear, confusion, sadness, or curiosity. Now, reframe it as the sages and mystics do: as a sacred transition, a continuation of consciousness beyond form. How does your inner council respond to this shift? What does your PFC understand about legacy and meaning? How does your Amygdala respond when death is no longer seen as destruction, but transformation? How might your ACC help balance grief with insight, and how does your Insula connect you to the sacredness of endings and beginnings?

Write about what it means to live—and love—more deeply by honoring the reality of death.

The Unity of Life and Death

Life and death are two sides of the same coin, intertwined in ways that are difficult for the mind to comprehend. As the ancient Eastern teachings of the Bhagavad Gita suggest, "Death is certain for the one born, and birth is certain for the one who is dead." This recognition of the cyclical nature of existence points to a profound truth: life and death are not opposites, but complementary forces in the dance of creation. Without death, there would be no life; without life, there would be no death.

In this light, life and death are not experiences that stand apart from each other; they are part of an unbroken flow of energy that transcends the temporal world. Life arises from the great void of non-being, and death returns us to that void, where we are ultimately reborn. This cyclical process is mirrored in nature itself—the changing seasons, the rising and setting of the sun, the birth and decay of all things. Every moment of life is pregnant with the potential for death, just as every moment of death holds the seeds of rebirth.

"How does my perspective shift when I see life and death as a unified flow?"

Reflect on a time when something in your life ended—a relationship, a chapter, a belief system—and something new emerged in its place. How did that transformation mirror the dance of life and death? How might your inner council—your PFC, Amygdala, ACC, and Insula—help you navigate the truth that death is not an enemy, but a sacred part of the whole?

Write about what it means to honor death as part of life, and how embracing that unity might help you live with more reverence, trust, and peace.

Understanding Death as the Great Liberation

Many spiritual traditions speak of death as a form of liberation—freedom from the limitations of the physical body and the transient nature of worldly experiences. The Buddha, in his teachings on impermanence, highlighted the fact that all things, including our bodies and minds, are temporary and ever-changing. To identify with these fleeting forms is to miss the deeper reality of our true nature, which is eternal and beyond form.

Death, in this sense, is not something to be feared, but something to be embraced as a natural part of the process of spiritual awakening. As the Sufi poet Rumi said, "Why are you so busy with this or that or good or bad; pay attention to how things blend."

The process of dying is not an event that stands alone but is, in essence, the dissolution of the ego, the ego that binds us to illusion and separation. It is through dying that we are made aware of our divine essence—our soul's immortality.

Death, therefore, is the ultimate reminder that we are not our bodies, not our thoughts, not our roles in life, but something far greater—a boundless consciousness that is connected to all that is. To understand death is to recognize the ultimate truth of who we are: not finite beings on a time-limited journey, but infinite consciousness experiencing a momentary human existence. In this recognition, the fear of death dissolves, and life becomes an expression of the divine—the sacred dance of spirit in form.

"What opens in me when I view death as liberation—not loss?"

Sit with the idea that death is not a tragedy, but a return—a sacred transition into something vaster than form. How does your inner council respond to this perspective? What does your PFC understand about impermanence and identity? How does your Amygdala soften when death is not an end, but an unveiling? Can your ACC help you hold grief and grace at once? And what does your Insula feel in your body when you imagine your consciousness as boundless and eternal?

Write about how embracing death as liberation might change how you live, how you love, and how you let go.

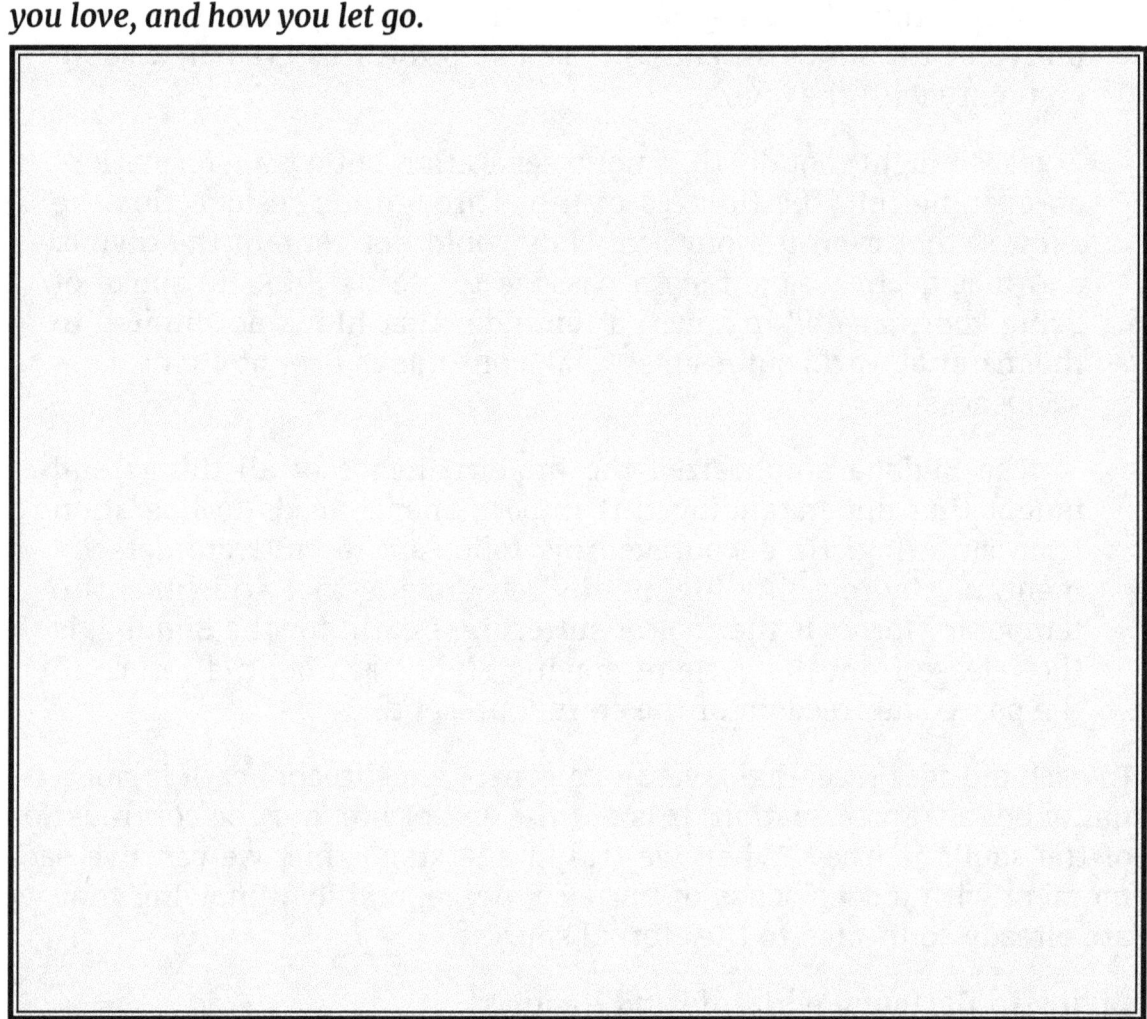

The Teachings of the Great Adepts on Death and Life

The teachings of spiritual adepts illuminate the relationship between life and death as a dance between form and formlessness, between limitation and freedom. The wisdom of sages such as Socrates, Jesus, and the Buddha invites us to live fully in the present moment, knowing that the impermanence of life is what makes it so precious.

- Socrates spoke of death as the ultimate test of our character, an opportunity to understand the nature of the soul. He believed that a wise person would not fear death but would instead welcome it as a continuation of the soul's journey. In his final moments, he embraced death not as an end, but as a step towards greater wisdom and unity with the divine.

- Jesus taught that death is not a separation but a transformation, an opening into the fullness of life. Through his resurrection, he showed that even the physical body could not contain the divine, and that death was simply a passage to eternal life. He spoke of being "born again" in spirit, a reminder that life is not limited to the material world but is an eternal, continuous flow of divine consciousness.

- The Buddha emphasized the impermanence of all things and taught that understanding this impermanence leads to liberation from suffering. He encouraged his followers to cultivate detachment, not by rejecting life, but by recognizing that attachment to temporary forms is the root of suffering. Death, for the Buddha, is the release from the cycle of craving and attachment, a return to the peace and freedom of the eternal present.

In each of these teachings, we find a consistent thread: death is not a finality but a transformation. It is not the end of life, but the continuation of the soul's journey. When we truly understand this, we can live each moment with a deep sense of purpose, peace, and joy, knowing that we are already connected to the eternal source.

Living in Harmony with Life and Death

To truly understand death is to live more fully in life. When we no longer fear the end, we can embrace each moment with grace and gratitude. Life becomes a celebration of existence—every breath, every heartbeat, every experience is seen as a gift, a precious moment in the grand flow of time.

The mystic's path, as shown by the great adepts, is one of unity—unity with the divine, unity with life, and unity with death. Death does not take away life; it adds depth and meaning to it. To live in awareness of death is to live in awareness of the eternal truth that underlies all forms, a truth that transcends the limitations of time, space, and individuality.

As we begin to perceive life and death as one continuous, interconnected process, we free ourselves from fear, doubt, and suffering. We are liberated from the illusion of separation, recognizing that we are both the flower blooming in the garden and the soil in which it grows. Death is not something that happens to us—it is something that happens with us, as an integral part of the life that we are.

"How does my life change when I stop fearing death and start honoring it as part of me?"

Reflect on how the awareness of death can bring more richness, presence, and depth to your daily life. When your PFC accepts the impermanence of form, when your Amygdala no longer panics at the idea of endings, when your ACC helps you balance love and loss, and your Insula roots you in the sacredness of the present—what kind of life unfolds?

Write about how death, rather than being the shadow of life, can become its mirror—helping you to live more fully, love more bravely, and be more completely here.

Life and Death as a Unified Whole

True understanding of death illuminates the true nature of life. When we know that life and death are inseparable, we awaken to the divine presence in each moment. The adept sees beyond the illusion of finality, recognizing that each moment of life is a living manifestation of the eternal. Death, rather than an end, becomes an invitation to dive deeper into the mystery of existence and to celebrate the infinite nature of the soul.

In this understanding, life is no longer a transient, fragile phenomenon to be feared. It becomes a sacred, divine journey—a journey that is not bounded by time but extends into eternity. When you live with the awareness that you are one with both life and death, you live with profound peace, acceptance, and an unshakable sense of the divine within you.

Embrace life fully, and in doing so, embrace death with open arms. For both are one—mirroring the eternal dance of the soul through this grand, mysterious universe.

"What wisdom arises in me when I see life and death as one sacred dance?"

Let go of the idea that death is the opposite of life. Instead, imagine them as lovers, as breath and exhale, as sunrise and sunset—each giving meaning to the other. How does your inner council respond when you live from this awareness? How does your PFC guide you with clarity, your Amygdala release its fear, your ACC hold the paradox gently, and your Insula feel the sacred pulse of existence in your body?

Write about what it means to live as someone who has already made peace with death—and therefore, someone who is truly alive.

CHAPTER 16

The Goal of Life: To Die Peacefully

From the moment we pop into existence, there's one thing we can count on—death is coming. It's the ultimate RSVP that no one can decline. But despite its certainty, how often do we really think about it? And even more, how often do we think about how we want to die? No, I'm not suggesting we spend our lives obsessing over death, but here's a little secret: the real goal of life might just be to die peacefully.

Now, before you roll your eyes and mutter something about being a "practical person," hear me out. I'm not talking about lying in bed one day, staring at the ceiling and thinking, "Oh, it's a good day for the great beyond." I'm talking about having a peaceful, calm, and graceful exit, which, believe it or not, requires a lot of effort while you're alive—especially in how you choose to live.

If we don't learn to grow up and create peace in our own minds and hearts, we're not just making life harder on ourselves; we're setting up the entire world for a chaotic time. If we want to die in peace, we first have to practice peace while we're alive. And let's be microscopically honest—how can we expect to die peacefully if we haven't even figured out how to relax on a Tuesday afternoon?

"What would I need to practice now in order to die peacefully later?"

Take a moment to reflect—not morbidly, but honestly. If a peaceful death is the ultimate graduation, what lessons do you still need to study? How can your inner council support you in this preparation? What does your PFC say about how you're directing your life? What fears might your Amygdala still be clinging to? How can your ACC help you stay balanced through joy and sorrow? And what truths is your Insula quietly whispering from your body?

Write about the connection between peace in life and peace in death. What tiny, tangible choices can you make—today—to create a more graceful, grounded exit when the time comes?

The Peaceful End: A Life Well Lived = A Peaceful Death

So here's the deal: the best way to prepare for a peaceful death is to live a peaceful life. Simple, right? But you can't expect to face death with grace if you're not living with grace right now. Imagine, just for a moment, the freedom of knowing that when your time comes, you'll be able to say, "I lived fully, I loved well, and I have no regrets." That's the goal, folks.

If you work on curating peace in your mind, heart, and soul while you're alive, the final moment of your life can be one of acceptance, not fear. You can exit this world with the same calmness that you carried through your days. Peaceful living means peaceful dying. And believe me, when that moment comes, you'll want to be as ready for it as you can be.

But let's look at the brain science again: a life well-lived is a life in which we learn to manage stress and reduce the physical and emotional strain on our nervous system. The more we engage our PFC and ACC in self-regulation practices, the less reactive our Amygdala becomes. When the Amygdala isn't constantly in overdrive, we don't build up that anxiety, fear, and stress that can accompany death. We can face that moment in a state of peace, knowing that we lived as we were meant to.

So, as you go about your day, remember this: if you're cultivating inner peace now, you're already preparing for a peaceful death. It's like building a house, brick by brick. You're not just getting it ready for the final inspection—you're making sure the foundation is strong enough to hold up for a lifetime. And when that lifetime ends, you'll be able to say, "I did my best, I embraced peace, and now I can let go, knowing I lived well."

And if all else fails—just breathe, stretch, and remember: you're doing great.

"What would it mean for me to live in a way that prepares me for a peaceful death?"

Imagine your final moment—not with fear, but with reverence. What would you want to feel in your heart? What would your PFC reflect on with calm clarity? Would your Amygdala be quiet, knowing you chose love over fear more often than not? How might your ACC help you hold gratitude for both joy and pain?

And what peaceful sensations might your Insula carry through your body as you let go?

Now reverse-engineer that moment. What does your life need to look like today—emotionally, spiritually, neurologically—for that peace to be possible? Write about how you're building that foundation now, brick by brick, moment by moment.

A Contrasting Criticism: The Aggressive Way We Die in the West

In contrast to the peaceful death we aspire to—one that flows naturally like the turning of the seasons—death in the West is often more of a wrestling match. In the modern world, particularly in the West, the process of dying has become a drama, complete with flashing lights, alarms, and the kind of commotion you'd expect at a high-stakes game show. Instead of being treated with quiet reverence, death is often fought, avoided, and monetized in the most aggressive ways imaginable.

Let's start with hospitals—the grand stage for our death-defying antics. Picture this: you're in the hospital, and instead of the calm, peaceful exit we all secretly hope for, you're greeted with the constant beeping of machines, the whoosh of ventilators, and the non-stop hustle of overworked staff. It's like trying to have a peaceful nap while a parade of marching bands plays on a loop outside your window. The peacefulness of the moment is drowned out by the frantic attempts of modern medicine to keep you alive at all costs. It's as though the whole system is obsessed with the idea that the only real victory is defeating death, even if it means ignoring the actual wishes of the person dying—or even their loved ones.

And speaking of loved ones, have you ever seen family members in a hospital setting when death is approaching? It's like watching a reality TV show where nobody knows the rules, and no one gets the ending they want. There's crying, confusion, and well-meaning attempts to prolong life with various interventions. It's understandable—no one wants to say goodbye. But we've been taught, as a culture, that we should fight for every last breath, even when it may no longer be the person's wish. It's like running a marathon when your legs are already tired, and someone hands you a baton you didn't even ask for. We're so terrified of letting go, we forget that sometimes, the greatest act of love is simply allowing someone to exit this world in peace, without the frantic chase to keep them tethered to life.

This fear often turns into lying to those that are dying. We tell our loved ones that they are going to be okay and deny them the opportunity of fully and honestly expressing themselves and their final beautiful reflections on their own lives. They are so close to merging into the beyond and our own fears drown out their voices of true clarity.

Enter the DNR (Do Not Resuscitate) order—the legally binding "hey, let them go already" card. But, here's the catch: it's not always so clear-cut. For many families, these decisions become emotional minefields. Do we respect the patient's wishes? Or do we follow the pressure of modern medicine that wants to keep the show running, even when the credits are rolling? It's a tough call, and one that often comes too late, under the weight of mounting uncertainty.

Then, of course, we have the monetary aspect of death—and no, I'm not talking about the free lunch that comes with every hospital stay. In the West, death is not just a personal transition, it's also an economic transaction. Let's talk funeral costs. The price of death these days is shocking. You can get a budget "sleeping pod" (also known as a coffin), or you can splurge on a designer one, decked out with all the frills. You want a traditional burial? That'll be extra. Cremation? Still a pretty penny. Oh, and don't forget the cost of the memorial service, flowers, and a shiny headstone that'll make you feel like your loved one went to the afterlife in style. But here's the kicker: this isn't even the real price—it's just a bunch of emotional markup added because society insists that death should come with a spectacle.

Let's be honest, the capitalization of death is alive and well, and it's thriving like an overzealous lemonade stand. Death has become a product—wrapped in shiny paper, marketed with "feel-good" slogans like "Celebrate Life!" and "Send them off in style!" We're so obsessed with the look of dying, we forget that it's not about how many people show up to your memorial or whether your urn matches your interior decor. It's about how we handle the transition—not the "stuff" surrounding it. But alas, we've turned it into an industry, and the funeral industry is cashing in while we're busy counting how many pennies we have left for a fancy casket.

Why This Aggressive Approach to Dying Does Not Serve Us

The heart of the matter is this: death is not something to fight, but something to gracefully accept as part of the life cycle. Yes, we're terrified of it, but this fear doesn't make it go away—it only distorts the experience. And by treating death like a villain to be vanquished, we rob ourselves of the ability to approach it with peace and dignity. When we turn the process of dying into a chaotic, anxiety-driven scramble, we risk missing the one thing that truly matters: the peace that comes with accepting the natural flow of life and death.

What we don't always realize is that in this struggle to avoid death, we often lose sight of the more important task: to live well while we are alive. After all, if we're constantly trying to outrun death, we miss out on the very thing that makes life worth living. Imagine running a race with no finish line, constantly pushing harder, faster, trying to avoid the inevitable. Wouldn't it be better to enjoy the scenery along the way? To find moments of peace, clarity, and joy right now, rather than waiting until the final moments?

This is not to say we shouldn't care for our loved ones when they are dying or that we should throw in the towel and let go without any effort. Caring for someone at the end of life is one of the most profound acts of love. But what we really need to cultivate is a mindset that allows us to approach death as an old friend—a natural part of the journey—not an enemy to be fought. And when we can approach death with that grace, we begin to understand that peaceful dying comes from peaceful living.

Reclaiming a Peaceful Death

Reclaiming a peaceful death means reclaiming the way we live. It means creating a life in which the inner noise and chaos are quieted—not by running away from difficult feelings, but by embracing them and integrating them with our own inner divine council. The PFC, Amygdala, ACC, and Insula—our brain's inner team—are not just there to handle life's stressful moments, but also to help us approach the final moments with grace. When our inner team is functioning well—when we've trained our mind and heart to be calm, centered, and peaceful—we can face death with the same serenity that we should approach any part of life.

In short, we can't expect to die peacefully if we've spent our lives constantly battling with our own inner world. Just like a great symphony requires all the instruments to play together in harmony, a peaceful death requires a lifetime of inner balance, calm, and acceptance.

And so, as we face the inevitable, let's make sure we're not just running the race to avoid death, but embracing it as part of the beautiful, mysterious cycle of existence. Life and death—two sides of the same coin, both worthy of our deepest respect. And maybe, just maybe, we can learn to live and die with the kind of ease and grace we all deserve.

CHAPTER 17

From Ego to Unity:
The Awakening of a Compassionate World

In every corner of our existence, the shadow of ego looms large. It is the force behind every system we've built—the governments that rule us, the economies that shape us, the schools that teach us, and yes, even the families that were supposed to nurture us. These structures, once conceived as means of unity and progression, are now shackled by the chains of self-preservation, competition, and separation. Ego, that whispering voice within, incessantly chants, "Me, mine, now." It drives our every move, our every desire, fueling the endless conflict and suffering that reverberates across the globe.

But fear is the true engine of this chaos. Fear of not being enough, fear of losing control, fear of the unknown, fear of the other, fear of death. We live in a world drenched in fear, a world where our politics are driven by the fear of losing power, our media is fueled by the fear of missing out, and our personal lives are shaped by the fear of judgment.

This fear is an insidious virus that infects not only our institutions but our very thought patterns, creating a web of reactivity. In this web, we become tangled in endless cycles of tension, misunderstanding, and confusion. The world becomes a battlefield, where every moment is filled with unseen enemies and imagined slights, where connection is replaced by suspicion and trust by skepticism.

The impact of this unrelenting fear is everywhere, a direct reflection of the chaos within. Our technologies, entirely capable of bringing us together, are instead used to divide us further, exploiting our vulnerabilities for profit. Social media amplifies our insecurities, spreading discontent like wildfire, feeding the flames of division instead of fostering connection. News outlets, driven by sensationalism and the hunger for profit, bombard us with stories of violence, corruption, and despair, leaving us feeling small, powerless, and afraid. Our economies, though brimming with wealth, are built on the backs of inequality, where the rich hoard their resources while the poor struggle in the shadows, unable to escape a cycle of poverty and desperation. Corporations dominate the landscape, treating the environment and the labor force as commodities, burning forests for short-term gain and exploiting workers in sweatshops across the globe.

And within us, the Divine Council—is divided, each part pulling us in different directions. Instead of being a harmonious system, they bicker and fight for dominance. There is no balance, no harmony. The inner world is a cacophony of voices, all shouting over one another. And when we cannot find peace within, how can we expect to create it in the world?

This collective ego—this pervasive belief in separation and fear—is not only out of control, it is destroying us. Our planet is dying in front of our eyes, as climate destruction ravages ecosystems that took millennia to form. Wildfire, floods, and droughts are becoming the norm, not anomalies. Climate refugees flee their homes in search of safety, only to face more hostility and fear in foreign lands. We are choking on pollution—oceans filled with plastic, skies clouded with smoke, and cities suffocating under smog. Our planet's lungs are being torn apart. This fear evolved to a point where we think that building a rocket ship and colonizing lifeless planets is more of a viable option than living on a planet beaming with life.

Meanwhile, social inequality has reached staggering proportions. Wealth is concentrated in the hands of a few, while billions live in poverty, without access to clean water, education, or healthcare. In cities across the world, homelessness is a daily reality for many. Families are torn apart by economic stress, unable to break free from a system designed to keep them down. Racism, sexism, and xenophobia permeate every layer of society, keeping people divided and unable to find common ground. We have created a world where the poor are blamed for their suffering, the marginalized are silenced, and the voiceless are ignored.

Mental health is at a breaking point. Anxiety, depression, and loneliness are now the global pandemic—affecting millions of people every day. People are overwhelmed, disconnected from their own sense of purpose, and caught in the spiraling storm of their own thoughts. Suicide rates are climbing, especially among our youth, who are burdened by the pressure of perfection, comparison, and the relentless pursuit of an unattainable ideal.

And yet, violence continues to escalate. From mass shootings in schools and malls, to armed conflicts in far-off lands, the drumbeat of bloodshed and destruction never seems to stop. Children are born into war zones, forced to grow up too quickly in a world that has already forgotten how to play. Nations spend trillions on weapons of mass destruction while ignoring the human cost of their decisions.

But here's the truth: This is not our destiny.

It doesn't have to be this way.

There is another path—a higher path, a path rooted in compassion, reason, and deep transformation. It is a path where we choose not to react, but to respond; where we embrace our inner wisdom instead of feeding the fear that holds us captive. It is a path where neurological and systemic independence becomes the bedrock of a new era—an era of collective peace and unity.

But this change doesn't begin with governments, corporations, or leaders. Let the pigs play in the mud. Don't get me wrong, pigs will be pigs and that is another way that life is experiencing itself. But this change begins with you. It begins now.

We have the power to begin this journey of transformation today, in this very moment. All it takes is the courage to choose balance, clarity, and love over fear. It begins within each of us, as we call upon our own Divine Council—our wisdom, our passion, our intuition, and our ability to find peace even in the most difficult circumstances. When we learn to harmonize these forces, we will not only change our lives—we will change the world.

This is our time. The future is ours to shape. The question is: Will we rise to meet it?

The time to choose peace is now. Write down all of the feelings that you might have toward this topic. Then sit with your feelings in peace and write down any changes you feel in your body and mind.

"What awakens in me when I imagine a world beyond ego, beyond fear?"

Let yourself feel all of it—the heartbreak, the anger, the overwhelm, the helplessness, the flickers of hope. Write down every emotion that arises as you read this vision of the world we've built and the world that's still possible. Let your inner council speak to each feeling:

- What does your PFC say about the choices you're making daily?

- What is your Amygdala afraid of—and what does it need to feel safe?

- How can your ACC hold both heartbreak and hope without collapsing?

- And what is your Insula sensing in your body as you sit with this collective truth?

Then...breathe. Feel.

Write again. What shifted? What did you release? What new truth or courage arose when you sat with it all without running away?

This is where awakening begins. This is where peace is planted. What world do you feel called to shape?

Neurological and Systemic Independence: The Only Way Forward

What if, instead of reacting in fear and ego, we could learn to master our inner world? What if we could call upon the wisdom of the Prefrontal Cortex, the passion of the Amygdala, the harmony of the Anterior Cingulate Cortex, and the deep intuition of the Insula to work in concert, creating clarity, peace, and alignment? What if we could choose to shift from reaction to response, from separation to unity, from ego-driven action to compassionate collaboration?

This is neurological and systemic independence. It is the ability to orchestrate the inner team of your brain, to quiet the noise, harmonize your inner world, and move through life with intention, clarity, and compassion. It is about aligning logic with emotion, intuition with thought, action with heart. It is about being able to stand in the midst of chaos and still maintain your center, not by force, but by the wisdom of knowing who you truly are.

When you cultivate this independence, the impact is profound—not just for you, but for everyone you encounter.

In a world governed by ego, bravery is not about "standing out" or "winning." Competition is the ultimate destroyer because there will ALWAYS be a loser. Ouch. True independence is about choosing to let go of the need for external validation. It's about choosing to align with your highest self, the divine wisdom within you, and standing firm in the knowledge that you are already perfect, already whole, already enough. Bravery is choosing to engage with life with an open heart, not in reaction, but in conscious response. It's choosing peace over war, collaboration over division, and love over fear.

It takes true courage to begin the path of neurological and systemic independence. Because in order to do so, you must first acknowledge the parts of yourself that are still ruled by fear and ego. You must face your own emotional triggers, your limiting beliefs, and your knee-jerk reactions, your own feelings toward your own inevitable death. You must begin the process of quieting the mind, not just in the moments of meditation, but in the midst of real life—when things go wrong, when stress arises, when the world tries to drag you into its chaotic rhythm.

But here's the thing: You are not alone in this journey. The Divine Council is always there, waiting for you to call upon them. The PFC, with its wisdom and clarity, will guide you in making decisions aligned with your highest good. The Amygdala, with its fire and passion, will fuel your drive and creativity, but without allowing you to burn out. The ACC will ensure harmony, helping you stay grounded and balanced even in the most challenging moments. And the Insula will connect you to your deep intuition, helping you sense the truth in every moment.

When you tap into this inner team, you create a system that is no longer reactive, but proactive. You begin to co-create with the universe, responding to life's challenges with calm, focus, and compassion. Can you see the vision?

"What becomes possible when I lead my life from the wisdom of my inner council instead of from fear and ego?"

Reflect on the current patterns that rule your reactions—moments when you seek validation, act from scarcity, or compete just to feel worthy. What parts of your Divine Council are being ignored or overwhelmed in those moments? What would it feel like to bring your PFC's clarity, your Amygdala's passion, your ACC's balance, and your Insula's quiet truth into alignment?

On the next two pates, write about the kind of choices, conversations, and creative expressions that would emerge if your inner world became a sanctuary of cooperation—not a battlefield of fear. Who would you become? How would your presence ripple out into your relationships, your work, your community? This is your shift point. Begin here.

CHAPTER 18

A World United in Wisdom and Peace

Imagine a world where every individual has fully realized their neurological and systemic independence. This isn't some distant, utopian dream; it's a radical reality within our reach.

Picture this: a global collective where every single person is aligned with their inner Divine Council—where their Prefrontal Cortex (PFC) is making decisions with clarity, their Amygdala is passionate but controlled, their Anterior Cingulate Cortex (ACC) is ensuring harmony, and their Insula is in tune with the wisdom of their body. In this world, each individual's peace contributes to the collective peace of the world. Each choice, whether big or small, is a reflection of wisdom, love, and understanding.

This doesn't just transform individuals—it transforms societies. When each of us is no longer at war within ourselves, we stop projecting that war outward. We no longer need to fight for dominance, to outpace or outsmart others, or to cling to outdated systems of power. Instead, we can collaborate in the spirit of unification, taking on the challenges of the modern world with creativity, compassion, and calm. Here's how this inner transformation would impact the world's critical systems, sparking an awakening of the highest order:

"What would the world look like if every person lived from inner alignment and peace?"

Close your eyes and imagine it—cities where conflict is resolved through dialogue, schools where emotional intelligence is taught alongside math, workplaces where compassion is the culture, and governments led by clarity instead of control. How would your own Divine Council contribute to this world? What role would your PFC play in shaping thoughtful systems? How would your Amygdala lend passion without aggression? What would your ACC do to harmonize complex human relationships, and how would your Insula help you remain deeply attuned to what really matters?

Write a vision statement, a prayer, or a detailed story from this world-united-in-wisdom. Make it personal—how would you live differently in this awakened world?

1. Technology and Innovation: Reimagining Our Tools for Good

Technology, at its core, is neutral. It is neither good nor evil—it is how we choose to use it. Right now, we've allowed technology to be hijacked by ego and fear: fear of losing control, fear of inadequacy, and fear of being left behind. This has led to exploitation, division, and a deepening of social inequalities. But imagine, just for a moment, a world where each technological advancement is made not out of greed or competition, but out of a commitment to serve the collective good. This is what happens when we bring our Divine Councils into alignment.

With the Prefrontal Cortex guiding us with clarity and rational decision-making, and the Amygdala fueling our drive and passion, technology becomes an instrument of regeneration instead of exploitation. Innovations aren't developed to exploit resources or create division—they are designed to heal the Earth, lift up the marginalized, and empower every human being. Imagine solar-powered cities, decentralized, open-source tech that's accessible to all, and systems designed to restore ecosystems rather than deplete them. The brain's balance allows for this: the wisdom of the PFC ensures that we remain forward-thinking, while the passion of the Amygdala keeps us committed to improving the world.

A world where technology serves the web of life—human and non-human alike—is within our grasp. And it begins with every individual choosing to align their inner councils in service to this greater good.

"What kind of world could we build if technology was guided by wisdom, compassion, and inner alignment?"

Imagine the tools of our age—AI, renewable energy, biotech, digital communication—being designed and applied not from fear or ego, but from a place of inner harmony. How would your own Divine Council approach innovation? What kind of inventions or systems might your PFC design if clarity and the collective good were the goal? How would your Amygdala's passion be channeled into creating rather than dominating? How might your ACC bring balance between advancement and ethics, and how could your Insula ensure that our tools remain deeply human and heart-connected?

Write your vision for a reimagined future where innovation becomes sacred—a reflection of our inner peace, not our inner chaos. What does that look like in practice? What role do you want to play in building it?

2. Agriculture and Sustainability: A Sacred Relationship with Earth

What if we treated the Earth as sacred, rather than as a resource to be exploited? Agriculture would transform from a business into a sacred practice. Imagine farmers who do not merely farm for profit, but with a deep respect for the land and the ecosystems they steward. When we access our Divine Council, we tap into a deep well of wisdom that transcends mere productivity. The Insula reminds us to listen to the Earth, to tune into the intuitive signals that tell us when the soil is tired, when the water is polluted, and when the air needs to be purified.

With our Prefrontal Cortex making thoughtful, long-term decisions, and our Amygdala fueling our passion for a better world, we stop treating agriculture as a commodity and start treating it as a co-creation with the planet. Through mindful, sustainable practices, we can regenerate the soil, replenish the atmosphere, and create systems of food production that nourish both people and the planet. What if every community garden, every farm, every crop was not just about feeding the masses, but about nurturing the sacred relationship between humanity and the Earth?

This could be the new agriculture revolution: one born from peace, sustainability, and balance.

"What changes when I see the Earth not as a resource, but as a sacred partner?"

Imagine yourself in direct relationship with the soil, the water, the wind. How does your Insula respond when you truly feel the Earth's signals? How does your PFC help you make choices that protect future generations rather than just today's profits? What does your Amygdala feel when it's driven by reverence instead of urgency? And how does your ACC help you hold both productivity and preservation in harmony?

Write about how a world rooted in reverent agriculture would feel, taste, and nourish. What would your role be in such a system? Would you garden, steward land, teach sustainability, or simply slow down to eat and live more mindfully?

Describe it. Let the Earth speak through you.

3. Mental Health and Wellness: Global Healing Begins Within

Our world has descended into a profound and expanding mental health crisis. Anxiety, depression, and overwhelming stress have become the silent pandemics of our time, affecting millions daily, often in ways that remain unseen and unheard. But what if we shifted our perspective?

What if mental health was not a battle to be fought, not a flaw to be hidden, but rather a gateway to transformation? Imagine a world where self-awareness replaced shame, where compassion dissolved stigma, and where mindfulness bridged the chasm of isolation. Instead of viewing mental health challenges as signs of weakness, we could recognize them as invitations—opportunities to deepen our connection to ourselves, to awaken to the truth of our own resilience, and to transform our suffering into wisdom.

Mental health is not simply the absence of struggle, but the presence of balance, clarity, and inner peace. It is the ability to stand in the storm of our own emotions without being swept away, to navigate the complexity of our minds with courage and grace. When we connect deeply with our own inner wisdom, we begin to uncover the roots of our suffering—not to dwell in them, but to heal them. Healing is not an isolated act; it ripples outward, touching the lives of others, shaping the world around us.

The Anterior Cingulate Cortex (ACC)—the sacred mediator of our Divine Council—plays a crucial role in this healing. It fosters empathy, helping us see ourselves and others through the lens of understanding rather than judgment. It guides us away from shame and into self-compassion, reminding us that our struggles do not define us; rather, how we choose to meet them does.

In this vision, self-care is no longer a privilege or an afterthought—it is an act of revolution, a fundamental necessity for every human being. The path to mental well-being is about presence. It is about reclaiming our inner world, cultivating clarity and balance through mindfulness, meditation, and conscious movement. It is about realizing that tending to our minds is just as essential as tending to our bodies. When we choose to heal, to care for ourselves with the same love we would offer to a dear friend, we are not just healing for ourselves—we are healing for the world.

And in this time of great change, the world is witnessing a surge of neurodivergent individuals stepping into their power, bringing forth new ways of thinking, perceiving, and creating.

You are not a mistake. You are a gift. You are, in every way, perfect as you are. Thank you from the depths of Life Itself for being who you are.

> If you are neurospicy, know this: you are not an error in the system—you are Life Itself's secret weapon. You are here to disrupt complacency, to challenge outdated paradigms, to show the world a different way of being. Your mind, your perspective, your unique way of experiencing existence is not just valuable—it is necessary. You were never meant to fit into a broken world; you were meant to help change it.

"What if my struggles with mental health are not problems, but signs of deeper wisdom waking up?"

How would you treat yourself differently if you believed your anxiety, sadness, or overwhelm were part of a healing process—not something to hide or fix?

What would your inner council say if they could speak with calm, kindness, and clarity?

Write about what it would feel like to treat your mind like a sacred space—not broken, but becoming.

4. Healthcare and Healing: A System of Balance, Not Profit

Imagine a world where healthcare is not driven by profit margins or the fear of illness, but by the desire to restore balance—holistically and compassionately. In this world, doctors, nurses, and healers would not just be caretakers of the body, but of the mind and spirit as well. They would be in tune with their inner wisdom, guided by their Divine Councils, and capable of offering treatments that not only heal the body but also nurture the soul.

Healthcare would be centered on prevention, wellness, and compassionate care. Rather than focusing on disease management, it would focus on cultivating health—a system that encourages individuals to take control of their own wellness through mindfulness, nutrition, exercise, and emotional regulation.

The Prefrontal Cortex helps develop a strategic, long-term vision for health, while the Insula provides the intuitive insight needed for truly holistic care. Healthcare would no longer be a transaction, but a sacred relationship between the patient and the healer, grounded in respect, wisdom, and empathy.

"What if healing was about balance—not just fixing what's broken?"

Imagine a world where doctors and healers listened to your whole story, not just your symptoms. Where your body, mind, and spirit were all part of your care. What would healthcare feel like if it were rooted in compassion instead of cost?

Write about what your PFC (clarity), Insula (intuition), and full Divine Council might design as a new way to care—for yourself, and for others. What would true healing look like?

5. Education and Personal Growth: Awakening the Divine Within

What if education was no longer about filling students' minds with facts and categorization, but about awakening their innate wisdom? Imagine a world where children are taught not just to memorize, but to listen—to their own inner wisdom, to the wisdom of the Earth, and to the wisdom of others. Personal growth would be at the core of every curriculum, with each student taught how to access their Divine Council from an early age.

The Prefrontal Cortex would guide their analytical thinking, while the Amygdala would help them discover their passions and desires. The ACC would teach them the importance of harmony, both within themselves and in their relationships with others. And the Insula would guide them to deeply understand their emotions and physical sensations, fostering greater self-awareness.

This would not only create a generation of thinkers and leaders, but a generation of whole human beings—individuals capable of shaping the world with love, compassion, and clarity.

"What if school taught us how to know ourselves—not just pass tests?"

Imagine being taught, from childhood, how to listen to your thoughts with your PFC, feel your passion through your Amygdala, find emotional balance with your ACC, and understand your body with your Insula.

Write about a new kind of education—one that awakens the whole human being. What would you have learned? How would students grow? What kind of world would that create?

The future of our world—of every human, every community, and every nation—is within our grasp. By unlocking the wisdom of our Divine Councils and aligning ourselves with neurological and systemic independence, we will not only transform our own lives, but we will set the course for a peaceful, prosperous, and just world. All we need to do is take the first step.

And that step begins now. Please. Stagnation is the scariest form that death can take while we are living.

The Time is Now

And here's the most beautiful part of all: This shift begins with you. Yes, you. The depressed, anxious, hyperactive, or whoever you think you are in the moment. Can you now see how all of these labels are potential traps keeping your awesomeness from rocking the status quo? Can you see how the fear of these "disorders" are just a tool for the few individuals "in charge" to maintain their own fragile definitions of success and control?

All of us are little specks in the Universe and for some reason we think that one speck has more significance than another. I invite you to show me which grain of sand is superior to the next.

You are the key to unlocking this future. Every time you choose to act from your highest wisdom, every time you call upon your Divine Council and step out of the ego-driven, fear-based patterns that have dominated humanity for so long, you are helping to create this world. Every small choice you make—whether it's choosing kindness, choosing clarity, choosing compassion over fear—ripples out into the collective, and together we will rebuild our societies from the ground up.

The courage to start this journey is the bravest and most compassionate act you can make—not only for yourself but for all of humanity. You don't need to wait for some grand moment of change. You are the change.

So, I invite you—step into your power. Trust your inner wisdom. Engage with life from a place of balance and peace. Your Divine Council is waiting for you to show up. The world is waiting for you to show up.

This is our time. This is our future. And it begins with you.

The time to heal the world is now.

CHAPTER 19

The Sacred Autonomy of Others

The Paradox of True Independence

We often think of independence as an act of separation—a breaking away from external influences, a declaration that says, I don't need anyone else to tell me who I am. And that's true, to a point. Systemic and neurological independence are about reclaiming authority over your own life, thinking for yourself, and breaking free from societal conditioning.

But there's a paradox at the heart of true independence: you cannot be fully free unless you recognize the full freedom of others.

Let that sink in for a moment.

Independence isn't just about your ability to think, feel, and live on your own terms—it's also about allowing others to do the same, even when their choices don't align with your own.

This is where so many of us get stuck. We fight so hard for our own freedom, only to turn around and try to manage, correct, or control the choices of those around us. We see a friend making decisions we think are misguided, and we feel compelled to intervene. We watch a family member cling to beliefs we've outgrown, and we want to wake them up. We encounter someone struggling with a challenge we've already overcome, and we feel an urge to push them toward a shortcut.

But here's the thing: freedom is not control. Even when we believe we're helping, trying to direct another person's path is a violation of their autonomy.

You can't demand independence for yourself while denying it to others. That's like fighting to escape a cage, only to turn around and lock someone else inside one.

Independence is a two-way street: if you want to be free, you must set others free too.

"What if true freedom means letting others be free—even when I don't agree?"

Think about a time you wanted to help or fix someone because you thought you knew better. What if, instead, your role was to honor their journey—even if it looks different from yours?

Write about what it would feel like to fully respect someone else's path. How would your PFC guide your restraint? How would your ACC help you stay compassionate? What would it mean to let go of control—and still offer love?

Holding the Vision of Freedom Is the Ultimate Gift

If you truly believe in systemic and neurological independence, then the most powerful thing you can do for the world is hold that vision—not just for yourself, but for others.

This is the real act of service.

Not forcing others to change.

Not convincing them to see things your way.

Not proving that your path is the right one.

But rather, embodying independence so completely that it becomes an invitation for others to do the same.

When you hold the vision of systemic and neurological independence, you radiate the permission for others to be free. You become a living reminder that people are capable of awakening in their own time, growing in their own way, and living on their own terms.

This is where real transformation happens—not through coercion, but through presence. Through the unshakable belief that every person is fully equipped to navigate their own life.

That is the deepest, most liberating kind of freedom.

And it is your gift to the world, just as it is yours to receive from Life Itself.

Freedom Is Not a Vending Machine

A lot of us, without realizing it, treat people like vending machines.

We put in time, effort, advice, love—hoping that, in return, they'll give us the response we expect. If we support a friend through a breakup, we want them to take our advice. If we share a book that changed our life, we want the other person to have the same epiphany. If we offer guidance to someone struggling, we want them to listen.

And when they don't? We get frustrated. Why aren't they taking my advice? Why are they making things harder for themselves? Why can't they see what I see?

But here's the truth: people are not vending machines. You can't just input wisdom and expect a perfectly packaged outcome.

People are wild, unpredictable beings, shaped by their own experiences, fears, and lessons. And no matter how much we think we know what's best for them, they have the right to their own process.

So what do we do instead? We shift from trying to control the outcome to simply offering without expectation. We give, we share, we support—without demanding that the person on the other end take a specific path.

Because real love—the kind that liberates instead of possesses—says: I honor your journey, even when it looks different from my own.

Holding Space Instead of Holding Power

There is a vast difference between holding space for someone and trying to hold power over them.

- Holding space means offering presence, understanding, and support—without trying to steer, correct, or manipulate.

- Holding power means trying to direct someone's path, even if we believe we're doing it for their benefit.

One of the hardest lessons of independence is realizing that no matter how much wisdom you've gained, you do not have a monopoly on truth.

What is right for you may not be right for someone else. The insights that changed your life may not be what another person needs right now. And the timeline of your evolution is not the timeline that others must follow.

So instead of leading, correcting, or convincing, try simply being present.

When someone shares their struggles, resist the urge to fix them. Instead, listen. When someone makes choices you don't understand, resist the urge to redirect them. Instead, trust their process.

Because here's the irony: the more we let go of trying to control people, the more they are drawn to us as a safe space for genuine growth.

The "Garden Gnome" Approach to Freedom

Think of life as a big, messy, overgrown community garden.

Every person has their own little plot of land, and they get to decide what to plant, how to arrange it, and when (or if) to pull the weeds.

Some people carefully plan every detail—straight rows, color-coded flowers, a Pinterest-worthy herb section. Others? Their garden is absolute chaos—random plants sprouting in every direction, a tomato vine climbing up a tree, and a mysterious patch of something that may or may not be edible.

Now, the mistake most of us make is trying to garden for other people.

We lean over the fence and say, "You know, if you just organized that better, it would be way more efficient." Or, "Why are you growing that? Nobody even eats that much kale."

But here's the thing: it's not your garden.

The best thing you can do? Be the friendly garden gnome.

- Sit in your own space.

- Tend to your own growth.

- And if someone asks for advice, sure—offer it. But don't force it. Don't start yanking out their plants because you think they'd be better off with more roses and fewer dandelions.

Your wisdom might be helpful, but their journey is their own. Period.

Draw your own garden. What would you grow? Why? Would it be allowable for another person to grow a different plant? Would it be allowable for another person to not do anything with their garden?

The Courage to Let Others Be Free

The practice of honoring another's independence is not passive. It requires immense courage.

It means relinquishing control, embracing uncertainty, and trusting in the innate intelligence of Life Itself.

Ask yourself: Am I giving others the same freedom that I demand for myself?

Write down your sincere response.

If the answer is no, then it's time to loosen your grip. It's time to stop trying to shape the world into something more comfortable for you and instead honor it for what it is—a vast, unfolding tapestry of lives, each thread weaving its own intricate story.

A World of Free Beings

Imagine a world where every person is allowed to be fully themselves—without judgment, without coercion, without the weight of someone else's expectations pressing down on them.

Imagine what it would feel like to live in a space where your choices, your beliefs, your very essence were honored rather than debated.

Now realize: you have the power to create that world, simply by living in a way that respects the independence of others.

Let people be.

Let them walk their own path.

Let them explore, struggle, fall, and rise again.

And in doing so, you will not only honor their freedom—you will deepen your own.

Because true independence is not about standing alone. It is about standing together, in full recognition of the sacred, unshakable autonomy of every living being.

When you embody this, you offer something far greater than advice, persuasion, or direction.

You offer an example. A vision. A possibility.

And in a world that thrives on control, fear, and limitation, your ability to hold the vision of true independence is the most powerful gift you could ever give.

That is the deepest, most liberating kind of freedom.

And it is your gift to the world, just as it is yours to receive from Life Itself.

Final Journal Prompt: You are free, what would you like to write about? Take some time with checking in with what you'd like to express. What is alive in you in this moment?

Growing Up!

Growing Up!

GROWING UP!
SYSTEMIC AND NEUROLOGICAL INDEPENDENCE

Gopal Das
WITH GAURI DEVI

www.ingramcontent.com/pod-product-compliance
Lightning Source LLC
Chambersburg PA
CBHW081428070526
44586CB00020B/2517